# ARTIFICIAL INTELLIGENCE

# European Health Management in Transition

**Series Editors:**

Federico Lega, Full Professor of Health Management and Policy, Director of the Research and Executive Education Center in Health Administration, University of Milan.

Books in the series investigate how changes to the health and social care environment are leading to innovative and different practices in health management, health services delivery design, roles and professions, architecture and governance of health systems, patients' engagement and all other paradigmatic shifts taking place in the health context.

The books provide a road map for managers, educators, researchers and policymakers to better understand this rapidly developing environment.

**Books in the Series:**

Federico Lega and Usman Khan: *Health Management 2.0: Meeting the Challenge of 21st Century Health*

Axel Kaehne and Henk Nies (eds): *How to Deliver Integrated Care: A Guidebook for Managers*

Federico Lega and Giada Carola Castellini: *Resilient Health Systems: What We Know; What We Should Do*

Federico Lega and Angela Pirino: *Developing and Engaging Clinical Leaders in the 'New Normal' of Hospitals: Why it Matters, How To Do It*

Federico Lega and Pia Kreutzer: *Building and Improving Health Literacy in the 'New Normal' of Health Care: Frameworks and Actions*

# ARTIFICIAL INTELLIGENCE: WHY AND HOW IT IS REVOLUTIONIZING HEALTHCARE MANAGEMENT


BY

ELVIRA BUIJS
*University of Milan, Italy*

ELENA MAGGIONI
*University of Milan, Italy*

FRANCESCO MAZZIOTTA
*University of Milan, Italy*

GIANPAOLO CARRAFIELLO
*University of Milan, Italy*

and

FEDERICO LEGA
*University of Milan, Italy*



emerald PUBLISHING

United Kingdom – North America – Japan – India
Malaysia – China

Emerald Publishing Limited
Emerald Publishing, Floor 5, Northspring, 21-23 Wellington Street,
Leeds LS1 4DL

First edition 2024



**British Library Cataloguing in Publication Data**
A catalogue record for this book is available from the British Library

ISBN: 978-1-83549-471-4 (Print)
ISBN: 978-1-83549-468-4 (Online)
ISBN: 978-1-83549-470-7 (Epub)

Printed and bound by CPI Group (UK) Ltd, Croydon, CR0 4YY

INVESTOR IN PEOPLE

# CONTENTS

# ABOUT THE AUTHORS

**Elvira Buijs** is a radiology resident at the University of Milan, Italy, and healthcare consultant. She earned a Master's degree in Economics and Healthcare Management (MIHMEP) from the Bocconi School of Management. As a Strategy Consultant with the Boston Consulting Group, she collaborated with healthcare companies, government agencies, and foundations across Europe and the United States. Her research interests are healthcare organization and management, strategy, optimization and quality of care. Her articles have appeared in peer-reviewed scientific journals.

**Gianpaolo Carrafiello** is a Full Professor of Radiology at the University of Milan, Italy, and the Director of postgraduate school of nuclear medicine. As an interventional Radiologist, he specializes in IR management of extra-vascular and vascular diseases. He is part of the review board of several important indexed journals, reviewer of numerous IR international journals and author of more than 260 articles published in indexed journals. He is an expert in highly technological interventions and has published several papers in the field of AI and radiomics.

**Federico Lega**, PhD, is a Full Professor of health administration at Public Health Department, University of Milan, where he holds courses in healthcare management and policy for medical students and leads the Research Centre in Health Administration (HEAD). A member of hospital administration boards and local health agencies, he is a consultant to regional health departments, national health agencies and insurances and the World Health Organization. He has been President of the European Healthcare Management Association (EHMA) and the Chair of its scientific advisory committee. Since 2015, he is the Editor in Chief of the research journal *Health Services Management* and an Associate Editor of *BMC Health Services Research* and the *Medical Care Research and Review*. He has published eight books and over 150 journal articles.

**Elena Maggioni** is a Research Fellow in health administration at the Research Centre in Health Administration (HEAD), University of Milan, Italy. She earned a Bachelor's degree in Economics and Management from Bocconi University, then a postgraduate degree in the management of healthcare organization and healthcare from the University of Milan. Her research interests are healthcare policies, healthcare organization and management, modernization and innovation in health service delivery, developments in competitive strategies in the pharma and medical device industry, chronic care management and clinical pathways integrating the hospital and the community.

**Francesco Mazziotta** is a Resident Physician in hygiene and public health, University of Milan, Italy. He earned a degree in medicine and surgery from the University of Milan. During the COVID-19 pandemic, he worked at a mass vaccination centre and in agencies for medical and hospital management and public health. His key interest is in how organizations can optimize clinical practice to improve the quality of care.

# PREFACE

## Reflections on Artificial Intelligence and Health Management: What We Know, What We don't Know, and What We Should Know

*Federico Lega*
University of Milan, Italy

The artificial intelligence (AI) revolution has begun. Yet, as in the early stages of all revolutions, we know the triggers and the promises, but we don't know much about current and possible developments, positive and negative collateral effects. Public and scientific debate is divided into two camps: the opponents raise an alarm about the potential risks of AI, while the advocates rally in boundless optimism about the unprecedented benefits that AI will bring to the future of humanity. Media coverage fuels the conflict.

A closer look at the healthcare and life science sector reveals both a positive and a negative side – there are high expectations that AI will bring improved accuracy, safety, speed and efficiency to clinical decision-making but also ethical dilemmas, operational challenges and wide-reaching changes in the labour market. The ethical issues are of particular importance, since AI applications for clinical use will need to weigh choices with complex trade-offs involving financial sustainability and cost-effectiveness. Studies have shown that AI can develop greater empathy than real physicians can; nevertheless, decisions on the best course of treatment for complex cases should not be left to AI algorithms, especially if we don't know which data the AI algorithm was feed. From an operational perspective, the central problem is supervising and controlling how, by whom, with what and when AI in clinical practice will be fed and trained.

Additional questions regard how many AIs can or should operate in a health system. Do they need authorization? Who has the right to develop them? Furthermore, how will AI affect the medical workforce and clinical researchers? How will healthcare organizations build their competitive advantage when AI applications are ubiquitous throughout a healthcare system (and yes, they need to be for the sake of equity), steadily encroaching on the professionalism established in years of personal study, practice, research and investment. How can life science change its inner dynamics of research and competition?

Presently, we do not know enough to answer these questions.

We know that AI performs better than real doctors, on average, in making an appropriate diagnosis and prescribing therapy in clinical decision-making. We know that its performance depends on how AI is fed and trained, as it will amplify biases present in the training data. For instance, distorted representation or unfair treatment of patients based on race, sex, language and ethnicity.

But we still don't know enough. We don't know how to manage the ethical issues AI raises. We don't know who will certify AI and how to counterbalance the agency's power. Who will decide who will feed it or how to design an authorization/

accreditation system for AIs in the health system or in a single organization?

We don't know how it will impact human resources for the implications for systems and organizations. What will the consequences be for countries like Italy, the United Kingdom, Scandinavia, Spain and Portugal where the public national health service is a major national employer, and the local health organization or hospital is the largest employer and driver of the local economy in some geographical areas?

These issues regard the political and the institutional environment, involve setting limits and authorization for the uses of AI in healthcare, responsibilities for its development and maintenance and means to guarantee equity in its accessibility and availability within the whole health sector. They should be on the agenda of politicians and authorities. For the governance of the health and life science sector. For the regulators and administrators of the system and the healthcare sector.

But these issues are not the focus of this book. Nor should they be on a health manager's strategy agenda. You won't find them addressed here.

So what can the reader expect to find? Everything related to the managerial responsibility of a hospital and health organization leader. Which is quite a tall agenda. Many aspects of AI that we should know and are often neglected or ignored by current research and debate.

If, for once, we turn away from the dominant perspective (and threat) of AI as a 'doctor' (or as a substitute for doctors, nurses or other health professionals) and try to envision its potential contribution to the management and the operations of a healthcare organization, we may then explore a new realm of possibilities. That's exactly what we should do and know. What we need to know if we want to improve the proficiency of healthcare leaders in managing the adoption of AI in their organization.

There are myriad potential AI applications that extend beyond clinical care decision-making to include improvement in organizational dynamics that AI can facilitate, support, enhance and augment. This is the focus and the core of the book, the key content of the research presented here. The work is centred on the managerial and the operational implications (opportunities and changes) for the adoption of AI by a health organization, from board room to bed side. The book was designed to provide health managers and decision-makers with a framework for action, grounded on solid analysis of theory and evidence. The framework is developed through the central chapters of the book, following the introduction to AI and before the final chapter on issues in AI implementation.

An overview of the book's contents is given in Fig. 1 which illustrates the diverse impacts of AI on a healthcare organization beyond the usual area of support or substitution in clinical care decision-making. In this perspective, AI can serve several different areas of organizational operations and management, such as:

- Support, redesign and improve delivery processes. For instance, AI can impact scheduling, staff labour division, technology maintenance and planning, among others.
- Support and enhancement of clinical management functions, e.g. risk management, clinical governance, clinical competence management. For instance, analysis of organizational data, building of casual interrelationships, continuous comparison with research evidence, gold standards and best competitor performance can provide valuable feedback to inform efforts to minimize risk, facilitate option of best-in-class practices, assure continuous customized training and workforce re-training.

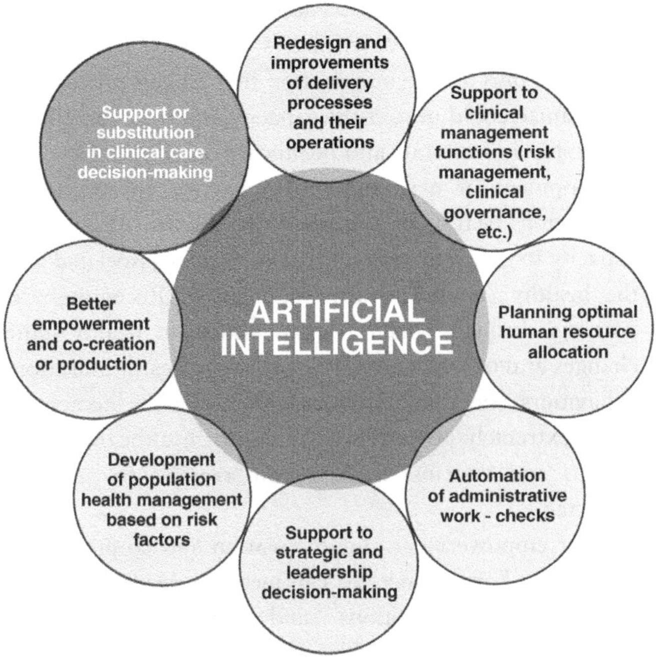


**Fig. 1. Potential Impact of AI on Healthcare Management Dynamics. *Source:* The author.**

- Planning optimal human resource allocation, from effective staff sizing and composition (skills mix) throughout a healthcare organization/hospital to planning short- and long-term recruitment policies.
- Automation of administrative tasks and controls. Bureaucracy can be substituted or managed more efficiently through AI, with improvement expected in speed, accuracy and streamlining. Whether the production of documents (e.g. certificates, clinical records) or payment management, substantial improvement can be expected.

- Support in strategic and leadership decision-making. Big data analysis, scenario writing, simulations, correlations, forecasts, plus all the information that AI can process and re-organize could impact the capacity and the capability of leadership in hospitals and healthcare organizations.
- Development of new and more effective approaches to population health management thanks to AI's greater capacity to generate and control risk factors associated with the healthy or chronic care population. Recognition of patterns through which AI can anticipate health status changes and/or new correlations between health indicators, behaviours, therapies, environment and health literacy can be an extremely powerful capability for healthcare organizations and systems to shift from reactive to proactive medicine.
- Greater empowerment and co-creation and co-production of services. For instance, AI can meet the needs of patients with chronic conditions and afford them better self-management of their illness. Alternatively, AI can support healthy citizens in maintaining their health through adaptive well-being behaviours and lifestyles.

All in all, AI holds promise for hospitals and healthcare organizations in their quest for better productivity, quality and sustainability. The development of AI for clinical use is well underway. The pharmaceutical and the medical device industries are competing for direct returns on investment in their business and for the chance to win a greater share of the current market or enlarge it (e.g. better adherence to therapy, risk factor control, prevention, novel therapies for rare diseases), whereas research and development of AI for management, operations and administration of hospitals and healthcare organizations lag far behind. Our case review presented here provides healthcare managers and top leaders with a glimpse of what the near future holds when AI is deployed to serve the management dynamics of their organization. Furthermore, analysis and framing of the impacts AI can have on administrative processes and on operations of clinical delivery pathways provide insights for managers and clinical leaders engaged in planning the adoption and managing the implementation of AI for organizational tasks.

Finally, the investigation of AI and its potential role in the evolution of health systems from reactive to proactive postures is enlightening and reveals an opportunity that policymakers, leaders and managers cannot miss. Nothing will be as it used to be. Nothing will be the same. On the verge of this revolution, we believe that leaders at all levels of health systems, organizations and hospitals should acquire a better understanding of AI if they want to guide its introduction, adoption and implementation effectively. It is our hope that readers will find the discussion interesting and take it as a call to action.

# 1

# INTRODUCTION TO ARTIFICIAL INTELLIGENCE IN HEALTHCARE


## ABSTRACT

Implementing artificial intelligence (AI) in healthcare organizations involves the entire organization. This groundbreaking technology is becoming central to achieve the goals of the new healthcare through the ongoing commitment to sustainability despite the severe lack of resources. Decision-makers in healthcare need knowledge and skills to prepare for the changes in many professional activities in the years ahead. Furthermore, chief medical officers and clinical leaders need to act on the opportunities that AI can bring, starting from its integration into the reality of healthcare settings while working with those responsible for managing and implementing AI in compliance with current legislation in Europe and the United States. Finally, stakeholders need to know how to leverage AI capabilities and how to recognize its limitations and its opportunities in administrative applications (admin AI) to optimize day-to-day operations and clinical applications (non-admin AI). In this view, clinical leaders and health care decision-makers may appreciate AI as a new way to provide sustainable social and healthcare services.

**Keywords**: Artificial intelligence; healthcare; admin AI; implementation; integration; opportunities; supervised learning; management; governance; reengineering

*Can a machine think?*

(Turing, 1950)

An unparalleled innovation of the 21st century, artificial intelligence (AI) is a major driver of technological growth, discovery and research. It can be defined as the ability of a machine or a software programme to perform cognitive tasks typical of human intelligence, like reasoning, problem-solving, pattern recognition and autonomous decision-making (eit Health, 2020; Russell & Norvig, 2016). Programmed to think and learn like human beings, it solves problems by drawing on extensive data sets and performs tasks that typically require human intelligence. Hence, the study of AI comprises diverse fields of knowledge that have converged to revolutionize technology and science, with the promise of transforming our ability to understand machines and their possibility to emulate human intelligence.

## AI IN HEALTHCARE: A HISTORICAL PERSPECTIVE

The history of AI is rooted in speculation by philosophers and mathematicians about whether the concept of intelligence can be applied to a machine or an artificial construct. Such ideas can be traced back to ancient legends. It is only since the 20th century, however, that AI has started to take shape and evolve into a field of research. The chapter's opening quote is taken from a manuscript written by Alan Turing, one of the 20th century's brilliant minds, mathematician, logician, cryptanalyst and computer scientist. During the Second World War, Turing used machines and computers to develop the Turing machine, a theoretical device that formalized the notion of algorithmic computation and laid the foundation for modern computer science and the Turing test, a criterion for determining whether or not a machine exhibits intelligent behaviour. Crucial to intercept and decrypt enemy messages during the War, Turing's work was a milestone in AI.

At some point in the 1950s, John McCarthy coined the term 'AI'. Economic resources permitting, research began to grow rapidly. In McCarthy's day, it was thought that machines could be taught to perform a variety of tasks: voice recognition, understand natural language, identify objects, engage in deductive reasoning and formulate new mathematical theorems. With hindsight, the founding fathers were onto something. In the 1960s, researchers developed programmes that could solve simple and linear algebraic problems, interact with people (e.g. Eliza Chatbot by J. Weizenbaum) and play chess in a challenge to the human mind, such as the DeepBlue calculator. But researchers also tried to teach robot to recognize and simulate emotions. The first was Kismet, a robot head with human traits designed by the Massachusetts Institute of Technology. Early applications of AI in healthcare can be traced to the 1960s and 1970s when AI systems were used to support medical decision-making in chemistry and clinical microbiology. The initial demonstrations generated enthusiasm, and the possibilities were just beginning to become clear. Although these were huge steps forward, it was not yet possible to consider them 'intelligent' machines because they were unable to detach themselves from provided inputs to generate outputs.

Thanks to the growth of computing power and the abundance of available data, AI has quickly reached ever greater heights. Moreover, software programmes can modify their own code using outputs derived from human inputs as inputs themselves. There are numerous examples in healthcare and other areas. For instance, self-driving cars work on a combination of sensors, cameras, radar and AI to read and react to external stimuli. The relevance of AI for mobility applications has attracted considerable interest, with car manufacturers investing in the market: it is estimated that it could generate a business volume of between $300 and $400 billion by 2035 (Deichmann et al., 2023). AI applications will then become exportable to other sectors. Intelligent virtual assistants (IVA), AI-based chatbots that interact with humans in conversation (e.g. Siri) and software that produces text and images that are difficult to distinguish from those created by humans (e.g. Dall.E, ChatGPT or Midjourney) are changing education, information, finance and accounting (Burns & Igou, 2019; Gubareva & Lopes, 2020; Liu et al., 2023; Priya & Sharma, 2023). Furthermore, AI has entered people's homes through the chips ubiquitous in household appliances (Caffo, 2023) like the smart refrigerators and washing machines that reduce energy consumption and waste. This progression is mapped in Fig. 2.

## DEFINITION AND CORE SUBSETS OF AI

The definition of AI might seem straightforward, yet it conceals intricate concepts and eludes even the scientific community. While AI, machine learning (ML), deep learning (DL) and neural networks (NNs) are frequently used interchangeably, each is a constituent of the preceding one and should be kept distinct from the others. To understand the differences, readers need to keep in mind what computer algorithms and computational models are. The former are coded instructions that take input data, perform computations and generate

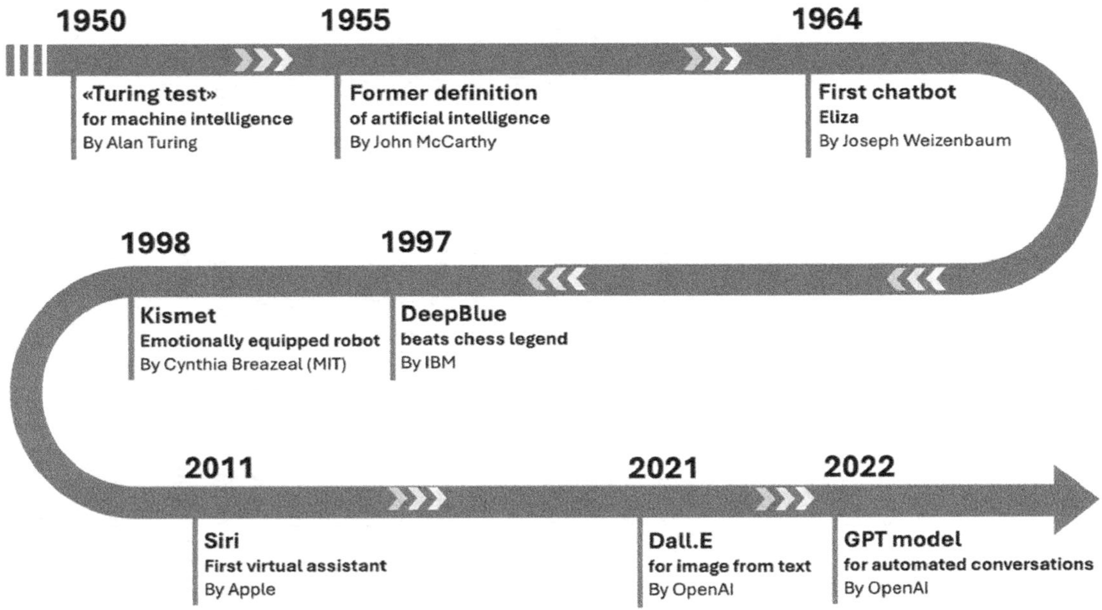


*Source:* The authors.

**Fig. 2. A Timeline of Progress in Artificial Intelligence Applications.**

output to solve specific problems, while the latter are mathematical or logical descriptions of how various components within a system interact with each other to produce certain outcomes. ML involves generating algorithms that enable computers to learn from data, make predictions or decisions without explicit programming, recognize patterns, extract insights and generate predictions autonomously. The data characteristics that an algorithm can be instructed to identify or that it can autonomously uncover are referred to as features. A key aspect of ML resides in an algorithm's ability to learn from the data itself with increasing effectiveness as it is exposed to more and more data.

NNs are computational models akin to the structure of biological NNs. They consist of interconnected nodes organized into layers that process input signals to recognize patterns, classify data and make predictions through learning. DL refers to the utilization of multilayered artificial NNs to model and process complex patterns in copious amounts of data, thus enabling machines to perform image and speech recognition, natural language processing and decision-making with high accuracy. A multilayered NN consists of layers of nodes between the input and the output layers. Each layer processes the input data and passes it to the next layer, with each consecutive layer building upon the representations learnt by the previous layers. Being stacked in multiple layers, a network can extract progressively higher level features from the input data, enabling it to learn more complex patterns and relationships.

ML falls under the umbrella of AI, where DL is a subset of ML, and NNs form the core of DL algorithms. NNs emulate the human brain by using a set of algorithms, while DL pertains to the depth of layers within an NN. ML relies more on human intervention for learning compared to DL (eit Health, 2020).

A hallmark characteristic of algorithms at the base of AI is that they can learn in a supervised or unsupervised fashion (Panesar et al., 2019). Supervised learning trains the system by labelling each input with its desired output value, while unsupervised learning generates inferences without the labels (Sindhu Meena & Suriya, 2020). This difference is important for the implementation of AI in healthcare since there are labels for some fields but not for all. Automatic classification of emails and price predictions are examples of supervised learning. Algorithms can aid in medical diagnosis through supervised learning, drawing on classification of inputs from clinical guidelines. Differently, algorithms based on unsupervised learning may help disclose insights into patterns, structures or relationships in data without the need to label them beforehand. This type of AI can be applied in population or patient segmentation within a specific setting. An overview of this is provided in Fig. 3.

Advanced systems for medical diagnosis and healthcare delivery support will be discussed in the following chapters. AI is a key tool in drug development, from drug discovery and design, identification of drug targets to prediction of adverse events and predictive modelling in clinical trials. AI can also

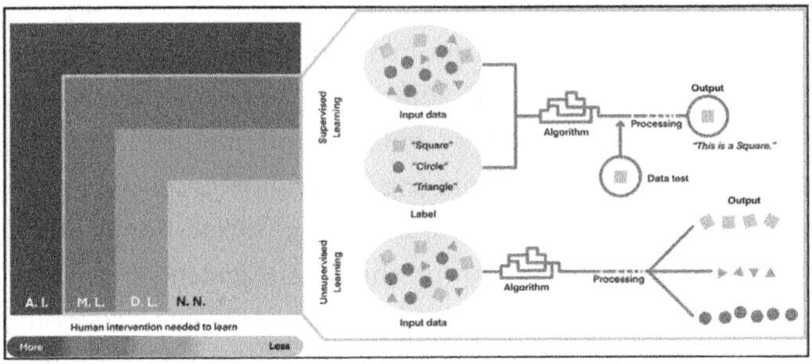


*Source:* The authors.

**Fig. 3. Overview of AI and Its Subsets.**

be applied to drug distribution and marketing (Vora et al., 2023), with clear advantages for the entire value chain for companies and patients.

## HEALTHCARE APPLICATIONS: A FRAMEWORK BY PURPOSE

AI has proven to be a game changer wherever implemented, and healthcare is no exception. Healthcare could benefit from the widespread integration of AI: improvement in the quality of care, shortened waiting times and waiting lists and alleviation of work-related stress, thus reducing the risk of burnout in healthcare workers. AI could optimize workload and provide support for continuous professional development, given the rapid advancement of medical knowledge.

For the purposes of this manual, we distinguish between non-administrative and administrative AI applications. The former are clinical or surgical in scope. Hence, non-admin or clinical AI provides diagnostic support, risk analysis of surgical procedures and risk assessment among other activities based on clinical data sets. Differently, admin AI refers to the optimization of organizational processes through the support provided by decision-makers in various settings and organizational levels. Admin AI supports workflow organization, choices dictated by activity volume and multiple variables affecting a particular context (e.g. epidemiology, sociocultural level, race) and the organization (e.g. professional staff). Admin AI can improve work shift management, outpatient scheduling, warehouse management and big data processing for reporting and other time-consuming or energy-consuming tasks (Chen & Decary, 2020; Dash et al., 2019; Houfani et al., 2022; Knight et al., 2023; Syed & Zoga, 2018). Such technologies can enhance the efficiency of healthcare delivery, streamline workflow and provide support for organizational management through predictive analytics of future events. Hence, admin AI generates solutions for optimizing processes that have an indirect effect on clinical outcomes (Mohanta et al., 2019).

Clinical applications of AI have been more widely implemented and investigated than administrative applications, since their effects on healthcare service delivery are visible and assessable. The immediate verifiability of an application generates greater choice of implementation by healthcare companies based on the simple evaluation of the same technology in benefits and usefulness. Both variables can be correlated with clinical outcome and internal (e.g. physicians) and external (e.g., patients and caregivers) satisfaction. Despite limited implementation often due to the longer timelines needed to measure the effects on the organization and the clinical outcomes, administrative AI applications' primary concern is resource efficiency and optimization. AI operates in the complex management of resources (people, time, money and goods), limiting waste of resources. Such complexities are compounded by the peculiarities of the healthcare sector itself. AI can be implemented in the management of an inconceivably huge amount of data. When applied to a healthcare organization's administration, AI optimizes resources, predicts scenarios and enables decision-makers to prepare in time, with a greater opportunity for patients to access services.

AI extends to all aspects of the clinic, from the production to the delivery of healthcare services and beyond. Many studies describe the new frontiers AI has opened in clinical medicine: support for surgeons in complex operations (Panesar et al., 2019); however, few to date report on the opportunities for administrative and management applications or leadership and decision-makers, although such applications mark a turning point in the production of health outcomes.

Time is a scarce resource but of fundamental importance in the clinic. A recent European study found that a large portion of medical staff working time is automatable or delegable, as it lacks clinical meaning and serves to fulfil administrative and bureaucratic tasks (Spatharou et al., 2020). Healthcare workers (physicians, nurses and social health workers) could benefit from automating the bureaucratic side of their work, allowing them to devote attention to their patients. In addition, automation could minimize the risk of burnout or loss of perception of meaning in work (De Hert, 2020; Lacy & Chan, 2018; Willard-Grace et al., 2019). Furthermore, a reduction of downtime for healthcare personnel and better planning of agendas through AI could reduce staff overtime and personnel costs. In brief, administrative AI provides an opportunity to manage human resources appropriately.

From a medical and administrative management perspective, many routine tasks are often largely automatable. Healthcare systems are striving to optimize processes (from diagnosis to administration) and resources to achieve sustainability. To do this, AI can be implemented transversally between units of a healthcare organization with a view to improve the quality of communications, clinical practice, multidisciplinary treatment and the actual and perceived quality of care.

## THE LEGISLATIVE, ETHICAL AND OPERATIONAL CHALLENGES AHEAD

Since AI applications are new to the complex world of healthcare, their regulation is difficult to establish. AI is rapidly becoming an integral albeit elusive part of modern life.

The potential challenges for legislators, policymakers, healthcare decision-makers and the entire supply chain (up to citizens) are daunting.

Europe and the United States differ in their approach to healthcare and innovation. In Europe, the General Data Protection Regulation (GDPR) is a legal benchmark for data privacy in relation to AI. The European Union (EU) is also developing AI-specific legislation to regulate transparency, accountability and safety. The United States has issued no federal legislation on AI, but various initiatives at the state level have been promoted, with a more industry-oriented approach and regulation regarding specific sectors. The US Food and Drug Administration (FDA) approved software for patient triage based on radiological images (FDA, 2023) in October 2023, reflecting attention to AI in administrative and non-administrative applications. Efforts in both Europe and the United States aim to balance innovation while protecting citizens' rights. Key issues include fairness and discrimination in AI, legal accountability, transparency and data security. Europe tends to follow a more proactive approach, while the United States tries to eschew restriction of AI development (Engler, 2023). Standardizing regulations internationally will prove essential to address global AI challenges effectively.

The absence of specific legislation related mainly to data privacy hinders AI implementation, whereas management applications not linked to patient data (e.g. shift scheduling) have been implemented and pilot programmes developed as for any other technology that cannot be defined as 'intelligent'.

The concern that the ethical aspects of AI will be at stake or compromised is real. In medicine, there is the dilemma of assigning responsibility for the decisions proposed by the machine: who is wrong in the event that the diagnosis is incorrect (the developer, the distributor and the doctor who relied on the information)? (Meskó et al., 2018; Santoro,

2017) And if the responsibility rests with the doctor who accepted the information provided by the machine, would he have made the same choice if he had no access to AI? To what extent does responsibility weigh on the choice to accept or not accept the use of AI?

Another criticality is the risk of bias and discrimination in AI systems, which results from the biases present in the training data. There is evidence for racial prejudice: 30% of Black patients wait longer for a healthcare service compared to other ethnic groups, and the phenomenon becomes particularly acute in communities with greater racial differences (Samorani et al., 2022). When AI is implanted in an organization, managers must first ask questions and adopt race-conscious goals, as well as test the algorithm before 'letting it think for itself'. This is one way to verify that the model reflects the reference population.

Moreover, AI-driven automation may lead to job losses and wide-reaching changes in the labour market, impacting on the local economy and social equity. Although the effect on job losses is difficult to estimate, 50% of the current jobs will be obsolete by 2030 (Frey & Osborne, 2017). These rapid changes require timely rethinking the models and topics addressed in training and university courses.

The inevitable task for legislators and regulators is to find concrete answers and start to address operational issues. Like other innovations, AI is developed via pilot projects and implementation attempts to overcome glitches in the set-up. The introduction of such a powerful tool, with the potent to replace human workers, requires due attention, sensitivity, professionalism and analysis of the context for it to be introduced effectively and efficiently. It is necessary to identify the appropriate niche, while setting limits and determining which tasks can be delegated and which cannot, in the understanding that human intervention can never be entirely and definitively replaced. Current knowledge dictates that some form of control, supervision and correction will always be necessary. From an operational perspective, the question arises about who is responsible for control: the doctor working with the software or the management or both? With what type of control? Who ultimately determines the quality of the AI output?

The task of strategic management is to identify transversality in the organization and possibilities of the integration of AI applications with what already exists. This risk may clash with the professionalism inherent to healthcare organizations. To solve this problem, the information may best be transferred via a top-down explanation of the strategic vision of implementing AI across the organization.

To conclude, the introduction of AI requires training of the personnel who will use it and identification of the infrastructure useful for its utilization, like new-generation computers, dedicated rooms and stable internet connections. Hence, a 'service design' effort may be necessary. This involves substantial initial investment and continuous reinvestment of resources to keep pace with developments.

Addressing these challenges requires a holistic approach to the ethical impact of AI and promotes the adoption of policies and regulations that ensure responsible and equitable use of the technology.

## HEALTHCARE LEADERS HEADING THE REVOLUTION

There is no area of healthcare where AI applications have no impact. Beyond the beneficial clinical and administrative changes that AI could bring to large-scale institutions, there are also possibilities for AI applications in private clinics and medical practices, with greater advantages in the reduced need for staff. In smaller facilities, the time required for activities is in comparison greater than in large-scale institutions due to the limited number of staff. However, this is somewhat offset by the proportionally smaller number of patients and selective case management often practiced by private clinics. In such settings, streamlining and automating the management of all administrative processes would provide a relevant advantage and improve the quality of care and the work of the entire staff team. The same applies to local entities (municipalities, schools, gyms, volunteer associations and community centres) that require greater integration between themselves and hospitals.

In all such cases, it is necessary to review the positions of the people responsible for the implementation of AI in both administrative and clinical applications. Although public health agencies are subject to budgets and plans for technology acquisitions, this does not apply to their implementation in the organization. Particular attention will be paid to the top management of organizations and operational levels to understand the most suitable organizational environment for the choice, development and correct use of AI. This may involve investigating which activities the operational and staff units will have to implement, from training to monitoring. Furthermore, given the specificity and novelty of AI, it could be relevant for healthcare companies to define an ad hoc role for this process (e.g. chief technology officer). Furthermore, training and communication are other elements for correct implementation. Chapter 5 will cover these new roles.

Moreover, to ensure sustainability, local leadership in the development of health technologies based on AI needs to be developed, adapted to the specificities of local contexts and favourable to the local population. The involvement of local government, academic institutions, research centres, international agencies, non-governmental organizations (NGOs), industry and civil society is crucial for developing and implementing such technologies (Siala & Wang, 2022).

The question remains about how a healthcare decision-maker can identify which activities can be assigned completely to machines and which cannot and in which ways can humans and machines be combined. This book will discuss the dynamics that allow for the rapid, reasonable and useful implementation of AI.

## REFERENCES

Burns, M. B., & Igou, A. (2019). "Alexa, write an audit opinion": Adopting intelligent virtual assistants in accounting workplaces. *Journal of Emerging Technologies in Accounting*, *16*(1), 81–92. https://doi.org/10.2308/jeta-52424

Caffo, A. (2023, August 31). Così Samsung usa l'intelligenza artificiale per ridurre i consumi dell'hi-tech in casa. *Il Sole24Ore*. https://www.ilsole24ore.com/art/cosi-samsung-usa-l-intelligenza-artificiale-ridurre-consumi-hi-tech-casa-AFXv5jh

Chen, M., & Decary, M. (2020). Artificial intelligence in healthcare: An essential guide for health leaders. *Healthcare Management Forum*, *33*(1), 10–18. https://doi.org/10.1177/0840470419873123

Dash, S., Shakyawar, S. K., Sharma, M., & Kaushik, S. (2019). Big data in healthcare: Management, analysis and future prospects. *Journal of Big Data*, *6*(1), 54. https://doi.org/10.1186/s40537-019-0217-0

De Hert, S. (2020). Burnout in healthcare workers: Prevalence, impact and preventative strategies. *Local and Regional Anesthesia*, *13*, 171–183. https://doi.org/10.2147/LRA.S240564

Deichmann, J., Ebel, E., Heineke, K., Heuss, R., Kellner, M., & Steiner, F. (2023). *Autonomous driving's future: Convenient and connected.* https://www.mckinsey.com/industries/automotive-and-assembly/our-insights/autonomous-drivings-future-convenient-and-connected

eit Health. (2020). *Transforming healthcare with AI.* https://eithealth.eu/wp-content/uploads/2020/03/EIT-Health-and-McKinsey_Transforming-Healthcare-with-AI.pdf

Engler, A. (2023, April 25). *The EU and U.S. Diverge on AI regulation: A transatlantic comparison and steps to alignment.* https://www.brookings.edu/articles/the-eu-and-us-diverge-on-ai-regulation-a-transatlantic-comparison-and-steps-to-alignment/

FDA. (2023, October 19). *Artificial intelligence and machine learning (AI/ML)-Enabled medical devices.* https://www.fda.gov/medical-devices/software-medical-device-samd/artificial-intelligence-and-machine-learning-aiml-enabled-medical-devices

Frey, C. B., & Osborne, M. A. (2017). The future of employment: How susceptible are jobs to computerisation? *Technological Forecasting and Social Change*, *114*, 254–280. https://doi.org/10.1016/j.techfore.2016.08.019

Gubareva, R., & Lopes, R. (2020). Virtual assistants for learning: A systematic literature review. In *Proceedings of the 12th International Conference on Computer Supported Education* (pp. 97–103). https://doi.org/10.5220/0009417600970103

Houfani, D., Slatnia, S., Kazar, O., Saouli, H., & Merizig, A. (2022). Artificial intelligence in healthcare: A review on predicting clinical needs. *International Journal of Healthcare Management*, *15*(3), 267–275. https://doi.org/10.1080/20479700.2021.1886478

Knight, D. R. T., Aakre, C. A., Anstine, C. V., Munipalli, B., Biazar, P., Mitri, G., Valery, J. R., Brigham, T., Niazi, S. K., Perlman, A. I., Halamka, J. D., & Dabrh, A. M. A. (2023). Artificial intelligence for patient scheduling in the real-world health care setting: A metanarrative review. *Health Policy and Technology*, *12*(4), 100824. https://doi.org/10.1016/j.hlpt.2023.100824

Lacy, B. E., & Chan, J. L. (2018). Physician burnout: The hidden health care crisis. *Clinical Gastroenterology and Hepatology*, *16*(3), 311–317. https://doi.org/10.1016/j.cgh.2017.06.043

Liu, N., Pu, Q., Shi, Y., Zhang, S., & Qiu, L. (2023). Older adults' interaction with intelligent virtual assistants: The role of information modality and feedback. *International Journal of Human-Computer Interaction*, *39*(5), 1162–1183. https://doi.org/10.1080/10447318.2022.2074667

Meskó, B., Hetényi, G., & Győrffy, Z. (2018). Will artificial intelligence solve the human resource crisis in healthcare? *BMC Health Services Research*, *18*(1), 545. https://doi.org/10.1186/s12913-018-3359-4

Mohanta, B., Das, P., & Patnaik, S. (2019). Healthcare 5.0: A paradigm shift in digital healthcare system using artificial intelligence, IOT and 5G communication. In *2019 International Conference on Applied Machine Learning (ICAML)* (pp. 191–196). https://doi.org/10.1109/ICAML48257.2019.00044

Panesar, S., Cagle, Y., Chander, D., Morey, J., Fernandez-Miranda, J., & Kliot, M. (2019). Artificial intelligence and the future of surgical robotics. *Annals of Surgery*, *270*(2), 223–226. https://doi.org/10.1097/SLA.0000000000003262

Priya, B., & Sharma, V. (2023). Exploring users' adoption intentions of intelligent virtual assistants in financial services: An anthropomorphic perspectives and socio-psychological perspectives. *Computers in Human Behavior*, *148*, 107912. https://doi.org/10.1016/j.chb.2023.107912

Russell, S. J., & Norvig, P. (2016). *Artificial intelligence: A modern approach*. Pearson.

Samorani, M., Harris, S. L., Blount, L. G., Lu, H., & Santoro, M. A. (2022). Overbooked and overlooked: Machine learning and racial bias in medical appointment scheduling. *Manufacturing & Service Operations Management*, *24*(6), 2825–2842. https://doi.org/10.1287/msom.2021.0999

Santoro, E. (2017). L'intelligenza artificiale in medicina: Quali limiti, quali ostacoli, quali domande. https://doi.org/10.1701/2829.28580

Siala, H., & Wang, Y. (2022). SHIFTing artificial intelligence to be responsible in healthcare: A systematic review. *Social Science & Medicine*, *296*, 114782. https://doi.org/10.1016/j.socscimed.2022.114782

Sindhu Meena, K., & Suriya, S. (2020). A survey on supervised and unsupervised learning techniques. In *Proceedings of International Conference on Artificial Intelligence, Smart Grid and Smart City Applications* (pp. 627–644). Springer International Publishing. https://doi.org/10.1007/978-3-030-24051-6_58

Spatharou, A., Hieronimus, S., & Jenkins, J. (2020). *Transforming healthcare with AI: The impact on the workforce and organizations*. https://www.mckinsey.com/industries/healthcare/our-insights/transforming-healthcare-with-ai

Syed, A., & Zoga, A. (2018). Artificial intelligence in radiology: Current technology and future directions. *Seminars in Musculoskeletal Radiology*, *22*(5), 540–545. https://doi.org/10.1055/s-0038-1673383

Turing, A. M. (1950). I—Computing machinery and intelligence. *Mind*, *LIX*(236), 433–460. https://doi.org/10.1093/mind/LIX.236.433

Vora, L. K., Gholap, A. D., Jetha, K., Thakur, R. R. S., Solanki, H. K., & Chavda, V. P. (2023). Artificial intelligence in pharmaceutical technology and drug delivery design. *Pharmaceutics*, *15*(7), 1916. https://doi.org/10.3390/pharmaceutics15071916

Willard-Grace, R., Knox, M., Huang, B., Hammer, H., Kivlahan, C., & Grumbach, K. (2019). Burnout and health care workforce turnover. *The Annals of Family Medicine*, *17*(1), 36–41. https://doi.org/10.1370/afm.2338

# 2

# ARTIFICIAL INTELLIGENCE AND HEALTHCARE APPLICATIONS


## ABSTRACT

Artificial intelligence (AI) applications are increasingly used for day-to-day operations in healthcare. Each has a relatively limited scope or task, and several find application in managerial and organizational processes. More and more, AI and machine learning (ML) devices have received US FDA approval in the last decade. This chapter covers the main AI applications in healthcare, with a focus on organizational AI solutions (administrative AI), the main AI developers, their investment and real-world data and case studies in healthcare and other sectors. AI can be applied in resource management and procurement, resource allocation, clinical case management, staff work shift scheduling and handling of emergencies. AI applications are becoming ubiquitous in hospital (e.g. emergency room and operating theatre) and outpatient settings (e.g. ambulatory care and dentistry clinics). Their implementation is expected to bring direct benefits for patient care and satisfaction. This chapter gives a broad definition of AI in healthcare settings, with a focus on administrative applications and their use in case study data.

**Keywords**: Artificial intelligence; healthcare applications; governance; management; administration; organization; hospital; clinics; patient care; outpatient

Healthcare systems are contending with rising costs, tight budgets, disease chronicity, long waiting lists and medical staff shortages. AI can play a crucial role in addressing these problems. AI applications are finding wider use driven by technological advancement and investment, with huge potential benefit for the healthcare sector. In response to wide-reaching transformations in healthcare, AI is poised to revolutionize workflows. For example, AI enables medical staff to devote more time to patient care by taking on time consuming administrative tasks that can be automated. Like many other applications, this impacts on workflow, on staff by minimizing the risk of burnout, and ultimately on patients by improving the experience of their healthcare journey.

## AI AND THE PROMISE FOR HEALTHCARE

The full scope of AI's potential for healthcare is yet to be understood; nonetheless, governments and the private sector are making substantial investment in the future of AI. According to the Statista 2023 report, the worldwide AI market in healthcare, valued at approximately $11 billion in 2021, is projected to climb to $188 billion by 2030 at an annual growth rate of 37% (Redazione Economia, 2023). From an economic perspective, providers in the healthcare sector can be evaluated by the amount of capital invested and the number of applications approved by national agencies (e.g. the Food and Drug

Administration [FDA] in the United States). A Future Health Index analysis, coordinated by Philips and conducted in July 2022, involved 3,000 healthcare leaders in 15 countries around the world and investigated trust in AI in healthcare. Sixty percent of global leaders and 56% of European leaders indicated AI as the principal focus of current investments. AI is and will be the top investment objective for directors of hospitals, private medical clinics, polyclinics and emergency medicine clinics (Da Rold, 2022). Furthermore, the number of FDA approvals has increased from two in 1995 and 1997, to a few more year by year, to 18 in 2016 and 139 in 2022 (U.S. FDA, 2023).

Another way to understand the magnitude of AI applications in healthcare is the political and legal action by national and supranational agencies. For example, in 2023 the European Medicines Agency (EMA) started an open consultation to gather input from stakeholders regarding the draft reflection paper addressing the utilization of AI in the life cycle of medicinal products to kick-start discussions with various stakeholder groups (European Medicines Agency, 2023). This shows just how aware Europe has become that AI cannot be overlooked but rather ought to be supported and regulated to control its development. China has also established its strategic development plan for AI in 2017, known as The Next Generation Artificial Intelligence Development Plan, with the aim to define strategic objectives, primary tasks and measures to support AI development by 2030 (Monreale, 2020).

## BIG TECH

Innovative tech companies have entered the healthcare market and attracted increasing interest from tech giants such as Google, Amazon and Walmart. They want to transform conventional healthcare approaches by digitizing services and disrupting the conventional provider-intermediated model (Deloitte, 2019). Hence, it is important to determine the impact of AI on how services are delivered, especially those with low complexity, e.g. activities that require a low skill mix or attention from healthcare workers for non-complex patients in outpatient services, day surgery or week surgery.

Many applications originally developed for purely recreational purposes are now found in medical applications. For example, Google Lens identifies skin rashes and gives preliminary information on skin conditions over smartphones. Google DeepMind was initially developed for video gaming; today, it is used for the interpretation of medical images (Balasubramanian, 2023; Dvijotham & Cemgil, 2023). Amazon Alexa started as an unpretentious home virtual assistant to become a telemedicine tool (Rae-Dupree, 2019).

Large tech companies are developing devices for the medical sector. In the collaboration between Google and the ophthalmology division of Novartis, Alcom signed an agreement with Google to licence the technology underlying smart lenses equipped with sensors, microchips and other non-invasive electronic components. Owing to their special 'smart' integration, they will have two medical applications: an additional visual correction for people with presbyopia, allowing them to read without glasses and restoring the eye's natural autofocus mechanism on nearby objects and support for diabetic patients by measuring glucose levels in tear fluid and then sending the data via a smartphone connection.

Another example of scientifically ambitious goals is Neuralink, Elon Musk's brain implant company, which could enable people with paralysis to control a cursor or keyboard with their thoughts. In short, well beyond the existing implants that can help patients carry out basic tasks with their thoughts. The first device was implanted in early 2024 and seems to work well (Sole 24 Ore, 2024). Although the outcomes will not be certain for many years, the expectations for this technology are high.

These real cases highlight concrete possibilities of AI in medical applications and opportunities for synergies between the private supply sector and the public and the private demand sector.

## UNDERSTANDING THE OPPORTUNITIES FOR AI IN HEALTHCARE ADMINISTRATION

Prerequisite to investigating the impact of AI on healthcare organizations is having a sound grasp of the conceptual background and logical categories of AI in healthcare. AI applications can be categorized into clinical and administrative AI. The former refers to AI for strictly clinical purposes and medical data, therefore needing approval from government health and drug approval agencies. ML algorithms, natural language processing and various other AI approaches are employed to analyze medical data. Healthcare professionals are provided valuable assistance in a range of responsibilities, such as medical decision-making, diagnosis, treatment planning and overall patient care.

Differently, administrative AI refers to technologies designed to assist in handling an organization's administrative tasks. This can involve natural language processing, ML and other AI techniques to streamline workflow and support administrative tasks and other organizational processes, such as scheduling, data and document management, and billing and reimbursement. Not all applications fit clearly into the administrative or clinical category, however. This is why hybrid software is employed to streamline administrative procedures and improve health outcomes. One example is triage applications that draw on clinical information but also streamline administrative tasks. Another is remote monitoring, by which administrative and management data can be collected by monitoring and evaluating clinical data.

Other AI applications can also be categorized by type of impact. For instance, AI can modify the relationship with patients and their networks (Healthcare to Patient, H2P) through the use of virtual assistants, remote monitoring devices, algorithms for personalized treatment plans and predictive models for disease progression. AI can impact on internal processes and/or supply chains that link providers, payers and regulatory bodies (Healthcare to Healthcare, H2H) without substantially changing the relationship with the patient, such as algorithms that optimize inventory logistics and drug distribution monitor and analyze production data to verify process quality. In H2P, the operational logics consolidated in an organization are modified, while in H2H the conventional organization and management models of healthcare are modified (Deloitte, 2019). The impacts and benefits of this are briefly overviewed in Fig. 4.

The current area of focus of AI applications is primarily clinical. In addition to applications in diagnostics, personalized treatment and data management, AI can facilitate virtual healthcare. AI-powered chatbots and virtual assistants can be

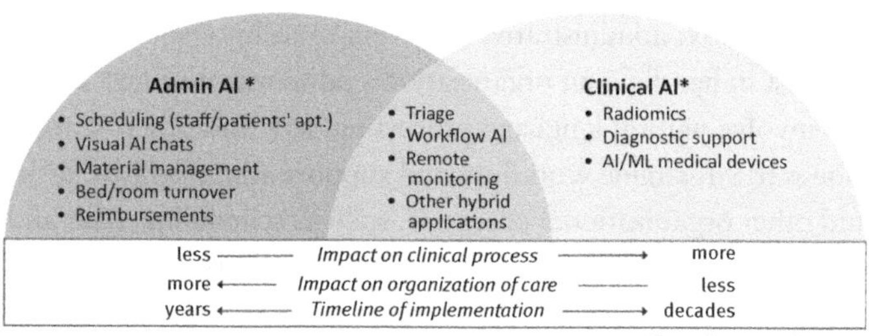


*Note: Radiomics refers to the method of the extraction of 'features' from medical images using data-characterization algorithms and AI.*

*Source:* The authors.

**Fig. 4. Impact and Benefit of AI Applications for Administrative and Clinical Purposes.**

used to collect basic health information, monitor a patient's health or provide emotional support via virtual reality (Swarnakar & Yadav, 2023). In this way, innovative therapies can be developed to address mental disorders or pain management (Ettman & Galea, 2023). Finally, AI can help in medical research by accelerating the discovery of new drugs and therapies, analyzing large datasets and identifying potential therapeutic targets (The Economist Editorial, 2023). A few examples are covered in Fig. 5.

AI can be viewed from different perspectives. The phases of the patient journey and back office activities of interest to decision-makers will be explored in relation to management. Current market developments and the supply chain will also be discussed.

## AI SOLUTIONS ALONG THE PATIENT PATHWAY

### Visual Chat and Virtual Assistants

The next generation of virtual chatbots for healthcare patient tasks such as appointment scheduling or other support are referred to as multimodal AI solutions. These artificial humans consist of a moving and speaking avatar that appears on a screen; they are enabled with the capacity for communication (verbal, non-verbal and paraverbal) to provide a suitable response in any given context. User emotions or non-verbal communications by patients are especially useful in healthcare settings, where a personalized touch can be essential, given the nature of the information exchanged (algho, 2024). The potential applications for a human-like virtual assistant are numerous. Though many are currently in development, benefits will most likely be found in enhanced effectiveness of scheduling, therapy adherence and patient satisfaction.

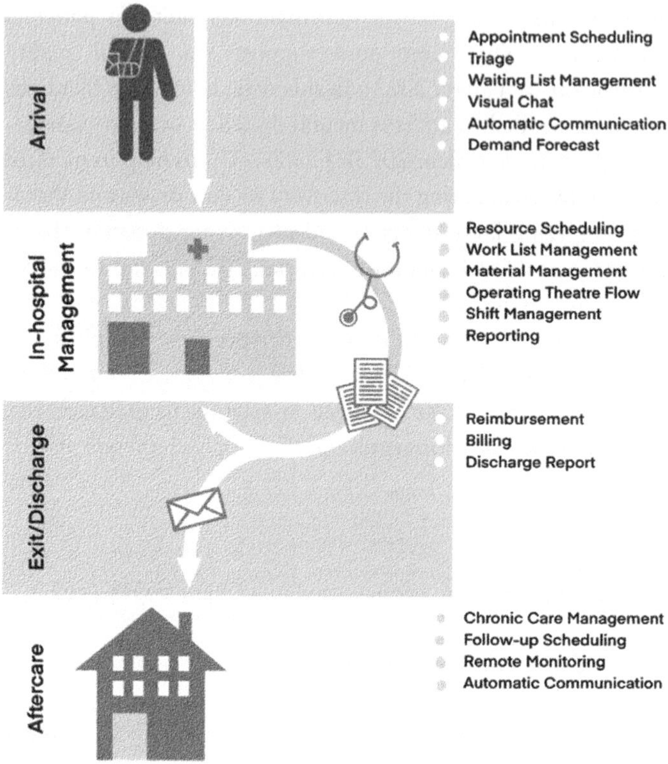


*Note:* Examples, not exhaustive.

**Fig. 5. Areas of AI Applications Along the Patient Care Journey.**

### Appointment Scheduling

The decision of when to perform a service is the first step in an elective treatment path. Scheduling is crucial from the perspective of the patient and the healthcare organization (Amigoni et al., 2023). For patients, delays in booking an appointment because of long waiting lists or delays in providing a service because of errors in completing a medical diary are common parameters for measuring healthcare service satisfaction and quality. The creation of bottlenecks is a source of multiple dysfunctions.

Bottlenecks can delay diagnosis and therapy, creating a series of further delays along a patient's care pathway, as well as barriers in access to healthcare services. A patient's health can worsen, resulting in higher costs and use of resources. Furthermore, prolonged dysfunctions can generate added workload and stress for healthcare personnel, compromising the quality of care.

Investigating the inefficiencies can reveal how central appointment scheduling is to management and clinical staff. Appointment scheduling is essential for the satisfactory delivery of healthcare services. AI application scan aid in optimizing appointment scheduling as follows:

- Demand forecast. ML algorithms can be used to predict peak demand based on factors such as disease seasonality, allowing for better preparation and scheduling of resources. This type of algorithms can collect historical data starting from hospital admissions, correlating them with meteorological models (temperature, humidity, etc.), demographics (age distribution and population density), plus relevant public health data (vaccination rates and prevalence of a disease in the community).
- Reduction of overbooking. AI can help reduce overbooking by accurately analyzing past performance and predicting the time needed for an appointment. Sometimes, however, overbooking is not an error, a mere systemic activity, but a necessity: in contexts where patient no-shows are high, a predictive model that minimizes the risk of collisions between appointments could increase patient satisfaction (Chong et al., 2020). Furthermore, AI can automatically estimate the time needed for a service by evaluating the

characteristics of individual patients. This will allow for better organization of diaries and increase patient satisfaction.

- No-show forecasting. Missed appointments are noted to increase workload and costs and to decrease access to care (Dantas et al., 2018). Using AI predictive tools, several studies have shown a decrease in costs per appointment and a decrease in no-shows (Chong et al., 2020).
- Customized booking. AI can factor inpatients' individual preferences, such as preferred schedules or special needs, to create personalized programmes that improve patient satisfaction. The algorithms of this type can be implemented with chatbots and virtual assistants.
- Automatic communication with patients. AI-based systems can automate communication with patients, sending appointment reminders, pre-appointment instructions and collecting additional information efficiently.

## Triage

The chronic overcrowding of emergency rooms (Savioli et al., 2022) may be solved by developing and implementing new methods for hospital management and rapid and immediate assessment of patients' clinical needs.

ML algorithms can quickly analyze medical history data reported by patients from crucial information about medical history, current symptoms and pre-existing conditions to help determine patient priority. Furthermore, through historic triage and diagnostic data and continuous updating the algorithms can learn to progressively improve triage accuracy over time.

Moreover, certain AI applications designed for triage have a high predictive capacity for complications or adverse events. The early identification of high or low risk patients can help rationalize the management of departments and assistance to the patients themselves in advance of clinical or laboratory test results, for which more time is needed (Chatzitofis et al., 2021). This allows for the optimization of internal hospital resources and the patient's therapeutic path, plus better resource allocation and general management of the clinical case and better management of the healthcare staff agenda and management of emergencies.

Finally, AI can automate the documentation of triage information while reducing administrative workload, thus allowing healthcare providers to focus more on patient care and facilitate collaboration between professionals.

AI will allow for different clinical governance of triage. Based on the scientific evidence present in the AI dataset, initial patient assessment can be carried out by administrative staff who, correctly trained, enter the patient data. This is especially true for primary care settings where patient needs are usually simpler. Furthermore, AI could provide for the same first level of triage by telephone or by monitoring data remotely. This, besides the benefits mentioned above, will allow for better governance of human resources, resources and spaces. In addition, AI should be monitored for efficiency and effectiveness by multidisciplinary teams to determine performance.

## Work Shift Management

Healthcare workforce shortages of physicians, nurses and technical staff are a major problem in healthcare. Chronic staff shortages make it difficult to cover work shifts, with operators often forced to work in suboptimal conditions (Boniol et al., 2022). To ensure that stress, fatigue and sudden absences do not compromise the quality of care and health outcomes for patients, medical directors should optimize shift management. It may also be argued, however, that personnel shortage is related to specialization with long training periods, which limits the implementation of short-term policies.

While shift management may be considered a purely administrative issue, it is one of the main determinants for the successful delivery of healthcare services. As such it can offer an excellent initial solution to medical staff shortage. Diverse work shift scheduling programmes are in place, but AI can offer certain extra advantages. Current software allows data analysis to inform decisions on the models, while AI can resolve problems by providing a solution. AI can be integrated into shift management software to improve the accuracy of labour demand forecasts, optimize shift distribution based on past activity patterns and suggest changes to improve the efficiency of shift planning.

Globus.AI, a Norwegian software scheduling company, claims that the increased scheduling precision afforded by its software allows hospitals to fill 40% more shifts (Davenport & Bean, 2022; Planerio, 2023). Several other work shift management companies are specialized in medical staffing though objective quantitative results are not yet available. Mobile-app and browser-based AI calendar tools allow for medical staff to directly communicate their availability and absences, whereas a 'superuser' has an overview and controls the staffing suggestions generated by the AI software.

Furthermore, the use of AI will verify whether employees are compliant with training and other elements of staff evaluation (Malik et al., 2022). AI can be used to design human resource management systems through the analysis of data extracted from CVs and external trends of staff satisfaction, a stimulus to growth and a reduction in turnover (Gong et al., 2022; Yang, 2022).

### Other Categories of In-hospital Resource Management

The primary areas of resource management are staff availability and patient appointments. Other areas of resources within hospitals and clinics that can be addressed using AI tools are:

- Patient flow. Prediction of patient admissions, discharges, and transfers, which reduces wait times and enhances resource utilization inpatient flow. Workflow can be standardized in clinical pathways, monitored and made more efficient thanks to AI. Patients are referred to appropriate services staffed by a multidisciplinary team (Dawoodbhoy et al., 2021). Here again, AI predictions can help.
- Surgery room time. Studies on surgical ward utilization have investigated shared optimized surgical bed and operating theatre availability. It is estimated that an operating theatre is among a hospital's most expensive resources, with an estimated cost of $22 to $133 USD per minute, while it generates about 40% of hospital revenue. A study found that ML effectively helped schedulers to more accurately predict actual surgical case length (Bellini et al., 2020).
- Hospital bed allocation. With the use of patient flow prediction, hospital beds can be better allocated and bed turnover and wait times improved. Moreover, the analysis of clinical data (e.g. vital signs, laboratory results and physician notes) can enable AI algorithms to identify patients ready for discharge, streamline the process and

promptly free up beds for new admissions. The AI administrator can also help eliminate incomplete discharge documentation so as to limit the number of 'bed blocker' patients. An example is the project at Kettering General Hospital, which will be discussed in detail in the following section.

- Inventory. Prediction of the use of medical supplies and equipment, facilitating proactive inventory management. This minimizes stock-outs, reduces wastage, tracks use by dates, optimizes procurement and ensures the availability of essential resources. Furthermore, the impact of AI on the hospital pharmacy will be analyzed in detail, as it constitutes a strategic sector in successful hospital management and holds a significant place in a hospital's budget.
- Predictive equipment maintenance. By using predictive analytics, AI can anticipate when medical equipment requires maintenance or is at risk of failure while dynamically prioritizing potential repairs. This proactive approach minimizes downtime of expensive equipment, extends usage and lifespan and ensures adherence to regulatory and hospital protocols for equipment management. It can also help prevent downtime and ensure that essential medical equipment is available when needed, thus avoiding disruptions to patient flow.
- Energy usage. Energy consumption can be optimized by analyzing use patterns and adjusting lighting, heating and cooling systems to obtain cost savings and sustainability objectives. AI enables energy managers to remotely monitor real-time indoor comfort conditions and control updated systems that effectively meet settings through advanced optimization strategies and facilitated by adaptive ML algorithms. An example of such AI models is a hospital in

Lombardy. An overall 8% saving in energy compared with the reference rate, which, if considered only on the perimeter subject to the optimization intervention of the hospital, would have reached approximately 20% of heating consumption (Frassanito et al., 2022).

## Administration and Reimbursement

Administrative costs refer to the non-clinical costs associated with running a medical system (Cutler, 2020). Their extremely heterogeneous nature makes it difficult to keep tabs on all expenditures in private and public healthcare systems. Administrative expenses account for a huge share of hospital budgets: 19.8% in the Netherlands, 15.4% in England, 12.4% in Canada and 11.6% in Scotland (Castiglione et al., 2015). Moreover, administrative costs in the United States averaged $2,497 per capita (34% of total healthcare costs) in 2017 (Davenport & Bean, 2022). The numbers warrant attention and call for a remedy.

The administrative activities that could be simplified with the use of AI are billing and handling of insurance agreements, plus other administrative procedures in human resources, legal activities, quality assessment, updating of electronic medical records (EMRs), customer support and credential management. The difficulty common to all these activities is the amount of information requested from clinicians, which then needs to be processed by the administrators. Moreover, since these activities are cumbersome and error-prone, healthcare systems need to standardize and simplify documentation and reporting, as well as data flow in order to simplify overall administration. In fact, administrative processes are among the most important and effective AI applications.

**Case Study**

The use of administration-oriented AI at Baylor Scott & White Health (BSWH) is a success story. The academic medical system comprises 52 hospitals, making it the largest nonprofit provider in Texas. Its goal is to reduce data collection costs, optimize net revenue and improve the patient's financial experience. Aiming to improve cost transparency for patients, BSWH introduced an automated, ML-based price estimator system powered by Waystar, a leading player in the healthcare technology industry. This system generates cost predictions before patients receive treatment, a widespread practice in many industries but unusual in the healthcare context, where accurate estimation of costs in advance is unusual. Prior to implementation of the tool, estimates entailed a highly manual process that required integrating data from various BSWH systems. A revenue cycle employee would normally spend 5–7 minutes to produce an estimate, albeit with limited accuracy. Presently, 70% of estimates are generated automatically, without any human interaction. In addition, discussion about payment options occurs before treatment, leading to a 60–100% increase in revenue at various service points in clinics and hospital departments. Doctors have expressed their satisfaction with the preventive provision of estimates, as this reduces the number of cancellations of procedures on the day of service. BSWH is also leveraging intelligent 'claims status' technology in the business office's insurance collections department to automate the process of checking the status of pending insurance claims (Davenport, 2021).

These applications also hold relevance at the systems level. An integrated network of applications developed at high levels of healthcare governance would allow for more accurate evaluation of activities and could aid in identifying semilegal procedures, such as 'upcoding bill' activities, in which a healthcare provider documents or codes a treatment or service with a billing code higher than the appropriate one in order to receive higher payment from insurance companies or the national health system. This practice is associated with excessive healthcare spending and may be considered a form of healthcare fraud if intentional. The implementation of these applications will involve hospitals and community care and primary care operators, since the new healthcare paradigms require new settings in which to focus healthcare (initiative medicine, care of complexities in the community and patient-centricity). These aspects will be covered in more depth in other sections. What is important, however, is to understand that countries with a national health service, such as Italy's, have more possibilities to intervene compared with Beveridge-based models (Rosano et al., 2013).

## AI TOOLS FOR HOSPITAL DEPARTMENTS

Besides AI solutions along a patient's journey, it may be interesting to focus on the use of AI in specific healthcare settings. AI can hold a prominent place in hospital (radiology, pathology and intensive care) and in outpatient settings (e.g. primary care, ophthalmology and dentistry). Given internal dynamics (e.g. lack of staff, resources and difficulties in procurement), AI applications figure among the main drivers of reducing direct healthcare costs in hospitals.

Numerous AI-based applications are being developed for use in emergency departments. One area is self-triage with English Babylon, the Australian Health Direct, the American WebMD and the Everyday Health Group. The latter comprises numerous specific applications for disease groups and conditions (pregnancy, obesity, growth and development). Other areas are emergency medical units (EMUs), in which AI assists emergency operators by analyzing a caller's speech and description as, for example in the Corti System, or the dispatch of ambulances with priority, like the Israeli start-up MDGo and the triage (Chenais et al., 2023).

Other AI applications in hospitals and operating theatres include its integration with environmental sensors to simplify the clinical load in a smart patient room. The Care.ai company implemented the Smart Care Facility platform. Furthermore, based on natural language processing (NLP) technology for data acquisition and ML sensors for activity detection, NLP interprets and transcribes doctor–patient dialogue, automates documentation and reduces manual input. ML sensors monitor patient activity and clinical processes to predict patient needs and identify anomalies. The Care.ai Smart Care Facility platform anticipates care issues by sending alerts and reminders to improve response in real time (care.ai, 2023). While operating theatres are subject to complex programming due to emergencies and complications that may arise during operations that go over the scheduled time slots, they incur extremely high fixed costs. The implementation of AI technology by Klinikum Stuttgart, a leading German hospital, in operating theatre management has significantly improved room utilization, leading to a 39% increase in planned surgical interventions, 30% greater accuracy in procedure duration estimates compared with standard methods and a 6% improvement in theatre utilization during basic operations. The algorithm, in fact, allows operating theatre managers to conduct data analysis by comparing planned surgical procedures with actual results, using ML to analyze 27 different variables (from a patient's body mass index to events the last time the surgeon performed a similar procedure) and predict the duration of the surgical procedure more accurately (GENTIGE, 2024).

Other solutions can be found in laboratories and radiology departments. To lighten the workload in laboratories, Aiforia has developed more than 400 AI models that integrate with laboratory software (PACS, LIMS, etc.) and support major scanners and file formats for image analysis. A single cloud for image collection creates a massive database with improved workflow efficiency and scalability, thus enabling new discoveries, better informed decisions, and more personalized patient care (Aiforia, 2023). Furthermore, the utilization of AI software in clinical data science and radiology practice is expanding in applications. Some notable instances of recent AI applications in radiology include the VIZ company's development of Viz LVO, an AI-based technology clinically validated for automatic detection and classification of large vessel occlusion (LVO) stroke, complemented by a mobile DICOM viewer. Another example is qXR, created by the Indian AI startup Qure, a tool designed to assist radiologists in detecting chest pathologies in X-ray images. Leveraging a proprietary deep-learning model trained on over 3.5 million X-rays, qXR can swiftly and reliably identify abnormalities in the lungs, pleura, mediastinum and bones in under 1 minute per scan (itransition, 2022).

The hospital pharmacy can also benefit from integrating AI into hospital workflows. There has been an impressive push towards personalized medicine in which treatment is adapted to the patient; this requires an update of pharmaceutical tools and methodologies. AI offers pharmacists the opportunity to automate repetitive tasks, reduce human error, provide targeted, patient-centred care and anticipate adverse drug reactions in susceptible patients. NLP and deep-learning approaches have been successfully employed in pharmacy practice to detect potential prescription errors and optimize medication management, while AI-based chatbots and virtual assistants improve understanding and patient compliance by providing detailed information and clear answers to their questions (Al Meslamani, 2023).

Also, the private sector is pursuing AI implementation strategies to manage their companies. An internationally recognized example is the IEO Biobank for Translational and Digital Medicine. Its peculiarity resides in its digital nature. Here, the physical material, composed of tissues, cells and biofluids, is digitized by advanced digital pathology techniques. This process links molecular data with digital data for optimal use of the most modern AI systems in technological research and development (IEO, 2023).

Moreover, AI can find application in many other fields for use by healthcare organizations. On the business side, AI can reduce costs and timelines for the introduction of new drugs on the market, which currently takes around 10 years in the pipeline and costs US $6 billion. Between 2014 and 2023, investments in AI by the pharmaceutical industry grew to a total of US $60.3 billion, underscoring the transformative potential of AI (Balocco, 2023). For instance, Coloplast, a Danish medical device company, uses marketing automation to communicate and support ostomy and catheter users, thus achieving engagement well above industry averages. Their personalized and interactive service programme is designed to help improve user conditions and quality of life with accurate and timely information via automated communication across multiple communication channels, including email, web, direct mail and telephone (Erickson, 2023).

Taken together, these developments constitute a huge opportunity for healthcare systems, whether public or private, complex facilities or clinics. Methodological clarifications are necessary, however, when AI is employed by an organization. One of the main risks in implementing AI in a healthcare organization is the duplication or unnecessary proliferation. Each of the multiple units within an organization needs to be able to develop autonomously. This means that each may implement its own AI applications independent of the others. To avoid such proliferation, however, a coordinator is needed to orchestrate between the units when they are carrying out transversal implementation projects and feeding the AI application with the greatest amount of data possible.

Moreover, healthcare policymakers and decision-makers will be able to use AI to dismantle the 'silo' logic that still characterizes many healthcare organizations today. To provide for the smooth implementation of AI, coordination should be overseen by a chief AI officer who will also handle the training of the people involved. The knowledge needed for implementing and maintaining AI as a profitable investment comprises core skills, digital soft skills and e-skills. Also, team leaders will need to possess leadership skills, i.e. the ability to make the best use of digital technologies within an organization and to introduce digital innovation into the market sector in which it operates (AgID, 2023).

Finally, patients should be involved in the co-production and the co-creation of activities and services, as well as in the implementation of AI. From the perspective of the organization, this entails a double advantage: greater trust by users and greater access to the data that 'feed' AI through stronger predictive models. Patients, physicians and administrators all have a voice in the change management process. The latter will be able to determine which steps of the process can and ought to be digitized. These factors will be discussed in more detail in the following chapters.

## REFERENCES

AgID. (2023). *Competenze di e-leadership*. Docs Italia. https://docs.italia.it/italia/designers-italia/lg-competenzedigitali-docs/it/stabile/doc/competenze_e-leadership/index.html

Aiforia. (2023). *About Aiforia*. Aiforia. https://www.aiforia.com/about-us

Al Meslamani, A. Z. (2023). Applications of AI in pharmacy practice: A look at hospital and community settings. *Journal of Medical Economics*, *26*(1), 1081–1084. https://doi.org/10.1080/13696998.2023.2249758

algho. (2024). *An immersive experience within your brand*. www.Alghoncloud.Com. https://www.alghoncloud.com/en/features/virtual-reality/

Amigoni, F., Lega, F., & Maggioni, E. (2023). Insights into how universal, tax-funded, single payer health systems manage their waiting lists: A review of the literature. *Health Services Management Research*. https://doi.org/10.1177/09514848231186773

Balasubramanian, S. (2023, June 13). You can now use Google lens on your phone to look up skin conditions. *Forbes*. https://www.forbes.com/sites/saibala/2023/06/16/you-can-now-use-google-lens-on-your-phone-to-look-up-skin-conditions/

Balocco, V. (2023, August 16). Intelligenza artificiale, ecco la prima mappa mondiale del pharma. *Corriere Comunicazioni*. https://www.corrierecomunicazioni.it/pa-digitale/e-health/intelligenza-artificiale-ecco-la-prima-mappa-mondiale-del-pharma/

Bellini, V., Guzzon, M., Bigliardi, B., Mordonini, M., Filippelli, S., & Bignami, E. (2020). Artificial intelligence: A new tool in operating room management. Role of machine learning models in operating room optimization. *Journal of Medical Systems*, *44*(1), 20. https://doi.org/10.1007/s10916-019-1512-1

Boniol, M., Kunjumen, T., Nair, T. S., Siyam, A., Campbell, J., & Diallo, K. (2022). The global health workforce stock and distribution in 2020 and 2030: A threat to equity and 'universal' health coverage? *BMJ Global Health*, *7*(6), e009316. https://doi.org/10.1136/bmjgh-2022-009316

care.ai. (2023). *Smart patient rooms*. care.ai. https://www.care.ai/smart-patient-rooms.html

Castiglione, V., Chiriacò, M., D'arienzo, P. D., Lauri, G., Malvicini, M., & Meola, L. (2015). *Le spese amministrative degli ospedali: confronto tra USA e altre 7 nazioni*. https://www.saluteinternazionale.info/2015/12/le-spese-amministrative-degli-ospedali-confronto-tra-usa-e-altre-7-nazioni/

Chatzitofis, A., Cancian, P., Gkitsas, V., Carlucci, A., Stalidis, P., Albanis, G., Karakottas, A., Semertzidis, T., Daras, P., Giannitto, C., Casiraghi, E., Sposta, F. M., Vatteroni, G., Ammirabile, A., Lofino, L., Ragucci, P., Laino, M. E., Voza, A., Desai, A., & Savevski, V. (2021). Volume-of-interest aware deep neural networks for rapid chest CT-based COVID-19 patient risk assessment. *International Journal of Environmental Research and Public Health*, *18*(6), 2842. https://doi.org/10.3390/ijerph18062842

Chenais, G., Lagarde, E., & Gil-Jardiné, C. (2023). Artificial intelligence in emergency medicine: Viewpoint of current applications and foreseeable opportunities and challenges.

*Journal of Medical Internet Research*, *25*, e40031. https://doi.org/10.2196/40031

Chong, L. R., Tsai, K. T., Lee, L. L., Foo, S. G., & Chang, P. C. (2020). Artificial intelligence predictive analytics in the management of outpatient MRI appointment No-shows. *American Journal of Roentgenology*, *215*(5), 1155–1162. https://doi.org/10.2214/AJR.19.22594

Cutler, D. M. (2020). *Reducing administrative costs in U.S. Health care*. Harvard University.

Da Rold, C. (2022, July 18). L'intelligenza artificiale, la sanità e gli investimenti. Cosa misura il Future Health Index? *Il Sole 24 Ore*. https://www.infodata.ilsole24ore.com/2022/07/18/lintelligenza-artificiale-la-sanita-gli-investimenti-cosa-misura-future-health-index/

Dantas, L. F., Fleck, J. L., Cyrino Oliveira, F. L., & Hamacher, S. (2018). No-shows in appointment scheduling – A systematic literature review. *Health Policy*, *122*(4), 412–421. https://doi.org/10.1016/j.healthpol.2018.02.002

Davenport, T. (2021, June 14). Improving the healthcare revenue cycle with AI and RPA. *Forbes*. https://www.forbes.com/sites/tomdavenport/2021/06/14/improving-the-healthcare-revenue-cycle-with-ai-and-rpa/?sh=20531f30122c

Davenport, T. H., & Bean, R. (2022, April 11). *Clinical AI gets the headlines, but administrative AI may Be a better bet*. MIT Sloan Management Review. https://sloanreview.mit.edu/article/clinical-ai-gets-the-headlines-but-administrative-ai-may-be-a-better-bet/

Dawoodbhoy, F. M., Delaney, J., Cecula, P., Yu, J., Peacock, I., Tan, J., & Cox, B. (2021). AI in patient flow: Applications of artificial intelligence to improve patient flow in

NHS acute mental health inpatient units. *Heliyon*, 7(5), e06993. https://doi.org/10.1016/j.heliyon.2021.e06993

Deloitte. (2019). *Prospettive, potenzialità, impatti e modelli dell'Artificial Intelligence in ambito sanitario*. https://www2.deloitte.com/content/dam/Deloitte/it/Documents/life-sciences-health-care/AI%20report%20medtech_Deloitte%20Italia.pdf

Dvijotham, K., & Cemgil, T. (2023, July 17). *Developing reliable AI tools for healthcare*. Google Blog. https://deepmind.google/discover/blog/codoc-developing-reliable-ai-tools-for-healthcare/

Erickson, J. (2023, May 5). What is hyperautomation? *OCI*. https://www.oracle.com/il-en/cloud/hyperautomation/

Ettman, C. K., & Galea, S. (2023). The potential influence of AI on population mental health. *JMIR Mental Health*, *10*, e49936. https://doi.org/10.2196/49936

European Medicines Agency. (2023, July 19). *The use of Artificial Intelligence (AI) in the medicinal product life-cycle*. EMA. https://www.ema.europa.eu/en/use-artificial-intelligence-ai-medicinal-product-lifecycle

Frassanito, R., Buso, T., Aumann, S., Toniolo, J., Albrici, P., Canevari, P., Iemmi, M., & Mapelli, F. (2022). How IoT and Artificial Intelligence can improve energy efficiency in hospitals - a North Italian case study. *E3S Web of Conferences*, *343*, 02001. https://doi.org/10.1051/e3sconf/202234302001

GENTIGE. (2024). *Optimize OR utilization with artificial intelligence (AI)*. GENTIGE. https://www.getinge.com/uk/insights/articles/digital-health/Optimized-OR-utilization-with-artificial-intelligence/

Gong, Y., Zhao, M., Wang, Q., & Lv, Z. (2022). Design and interactive performance of human resource management system based on artificial intelligence. *PLoS One*, *17*(1), e0262398. https://doi.org/10.1371/journal.pone.0262398

IEO. (2023). *Unità di Biobanca*. Istituto Europeo Di Oncologia. https://www.ieo.it/it/CHI-SIAMO/Come-siamo-organizzati/Le-divisioni/Biobanca-BIOUN/

itransition. (2022, November 23). *AI in radiology: Top 10 use cases and best practices*. itransition. https://www.itransition.com/ai/radiology#:~:text=Radiology%20is%20a%20medical%20specialty,which%20boosted%20their%20widespread%20adoption

Malik, A., Thevisuthan, P., & De Sliva, T. (2022). *Artificial intelligence, employee engagement, experience, and HRM* (pp. 171–184). https://doi.org/10.1007/978-3-030-90955-0_16

Monreale, A. (2020). Ethical and legal risks of artificial intelligence. *DPCE Online*, *44*(3), 3391–3397.

PLANERIO. (2023). *Intelligent shift scheduling at the touch of a button*. PLANERIO. https://planerio.com/

Rae-Dupree, J. (2019, June 29). Doctor Alexa will see you now: Is Amazon primed to come to your rescue? *FIERCE Healthcare*. https://www.fiercehealthcare.com/tech/doctor-alexa-will-see-you-now-amazon-primed-to-come-to-your-rescue

Redazione Economia. (2023, October 13). Sanità, minori costi e tempi di diagnosi: così l'IA può salvare oltre 250 mila vite all'anno. *L'Economia*. https://www.corriere.it/economia/innovazione/intelligenza-artificiale/23_ottobre_13/sanita-minori-costi-tempi-diagnosi-cosi-l-ia-puo-salvare-oltre-250-mila-vite-all-anno-3d2ca712-68e3-11ee-9c9c-ce3429611a2 d.shtml#:~:text=L'analisi%20dei%20dati%20pu%C3%B2,250%20mila%20vite%20ogni%20anno

Rosano, A., Peschel, P., Kugler, J., Ricciardi, W., Guasticchi, G., & Van Der Zee, J. (2013). Preventable hospitalization and the role of primary care: A comparison between Italy and Germany. *Journal of Public Health*, *21*(5), 445–454. https://doi.org/10.1007/s10389-013-0563-x

Savioli, G., Ceresa, I. F., Gri, N., Bavestrello Piccini, G., Longhitano, Y., Zanza, C., Piccioni, A., Esposito, C., Ricevuti, G., & Bressan, M. A. (2022). Emergency department overcrowding: Understanding the factors to find corresponding solutions. *Journal of Personalized Medicine*, *12*(2), 279. https://doi.org/10.3390/jpm12020279

Sole 24 Ore. (2024, January 30). Musk: 'Eseguito il primo impianto Neuralink nel cervello di un essere umano'. *Il Sole 24 Ore*. https://www.ilsole24ore.com/art/musk-eseguito-primo-impianto-neuralink-cervello-un-essere-umano-AFWIL8WC

Swarnakar, R., & Yadav, S. L. (2023). Artificial intelligence and machine learning in motor recovery: A rehabilitation medicine perspective. *World Journal of Clinical Cases*, *11*(29), 7258–7260. https://doi.org/10.12998/wjcc.v11.i29.7258

The Economist Editorial. (2023, July 13). Big pharma is warming to the potential of AI. *The Economist*. https://www.livemint.com/ai/artificial-intelligence/big-pharma-is-warming-to-the-potential-of-ai-11694423061504.html

U.S. FDA. (2023, October 19). *Artificial intelligence and machine learning (AI/ML)-Enabled medical devices*. https://www.fda.gov/medical-devices/software-medical-device-samd/artificial-intelligence-and-machine-learning-aiml-enabled-medical-devices

Yang, Y. (2022). Artificial intelligence-based organizational human resource management and operation system. *Frontiers in Psychology*, *13*. https://doi.org/10.3389/fpsyg.2022.962291

# 3

# AI APPLICATIONS IN THE NEW ERA OF HEALTHCARE AND COMMUNITY CARE


## ABSTRACT

The complex challenges facing the healthcare sector call for a revision of the ways it can provide high-quality services with economic sustainability. Revision can proceed along different pathways. Among the new paradigms of healthcare is the shift from a silo approach by hospitals towards an integrated, multidisciplinary approach. This entails restructuring hospitals in disease centres and exploring how AI can aid in the integration of hospital services and community care. Reorganization is vital to the development of patient-centred healthcare and the holistic approach. To achieve these goals, healthcare and policy decision-makers need to consider both the administrative and the clinical aspects of everyday issues. AI can play a key role in helping balance this duality. The overarching objective is to create interdisciplinary therapeutic and diagnostic pathways within care networks shared between the hospital and the community. This involves the analysis of huge amounts of data and interdisciplinary knowledge beyond the grasp of an individual. Therefore, knowing how AI can help in the development and reorganization of community healthcare is essential for clinical leaders to take advantage of this enormous opportunity in larger settings.

**Keywords:** Artificial intelligence; population health management; hospital reorganization; hospital–community integration; public health; integration of services; community healthcare; home care; new healthcare paradigms

## ARTIFICIAL INTELLIGENCE (AI) AND HOSPITAL REORGANIZATION: FROM SILOS TO INTERCONNECTEDNESS

Conventional hospital care is organized in silos, where units work in relative isolation from one another and collaborate little. Such an organizational structure can lead to inefficiencies, suboptimal patient care and reluctance to adapting to the complexities of modern healthcare. The fragmented patient flows can ensue in treatment delays, redundancies and lack of continuity in care. Furthermore, siloed structures can foster resistance to change and innovation. Departments may be hesitant to adopt new technologies or processes for streamlining workflows to improve overall patient care.

AI can play a transformative role by eliminating data barriers, fostering collaboration and thus optimize workflows across specialties. A more cohesive and interconnected healthcare ecosystem can benefit both healthcare workers and their patients.

How can AI help organizations adopt a multidisciplinary approach to patient care in a system so resistant to change?

AI can support data sharing and integration by merging and evaluating data derived from a diverse array of sources: electronic health records (EHR), diagnostic images, wearable devices and social determinants of health. Multisource information can be used to better understand a patient's medical and social situations, needs and preferences (Alowais et al., 2023), thus enabling health managers to build better business models and delivery systems for their organizations.

Also, data sharing can aid in interdisciplinary decision support, as AI systems can inform clinical decision-making based on best available evidence with the support of medical imaging software. A common platform can facilitate communication between healthcare worker (doctors, nurses and technicians) and coordination of patient care (Mittelstadt, 2022). An overview of this is displayed in Fig. 6.

Community care is undergoing wide-reaching transformations as the paradigms of modern medicine evolve, and the insights gained from the COVID-19 pandemic are put into practice. When addressing community health service reorganization, healthcare managers and decision-makers will need to identify key areas of clinical outcomes and administrative

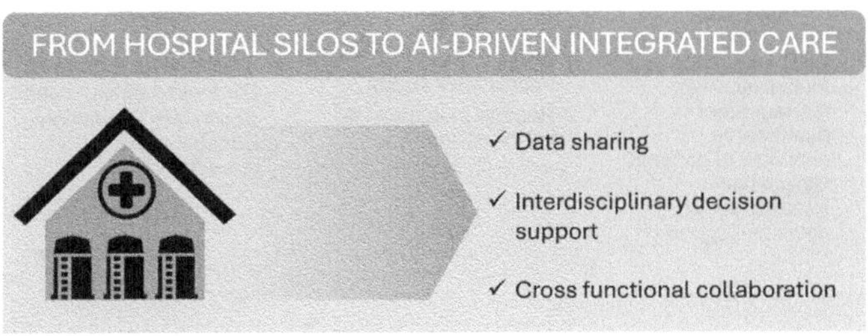


*Source:* The authors.

**Fig. 6. AI and Integrated Care.**

AI applications where the organization can benefit, and clinical outcomes be improved. Indeed, there exists a reciprocal relationship between transformation of the healthcare system and evolution of the AI market. Fig. 7 provides an example.

## POPULATION HEALTH MANAGEMENT

Population health management (PHM) is a crucial factor in value-based care where quality comes before quantity. It marks a shift from reactive healthcare to a proactive, preventive strategy for community well-being. In today's healthcare landscape, PHM aligns with value-based care goals, thus containing costs, addressing health disparities, emphasizing prevention, engaging patients, leveraging technologies and tackling global health challenges. This change towards a proactive, patient-centred healthcare paradigm recognizes individual patient needs within the broader context of community health.

For PHM initiatives to effectively reach their target, data play a crucial role. Data collected from diverse sources (e.g. EHRs,

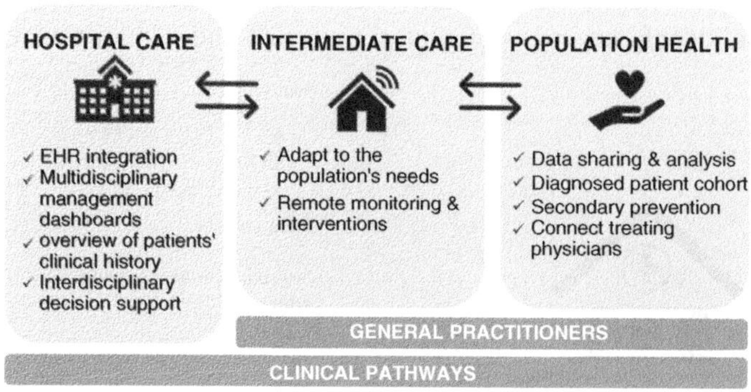


*Source:* The authors.

**Fig. 7. AI and Care Settings.**

claims, public health databases and social determinants of health) need to be merged to obtain a comprehensive understanding of a population's health needs, clinical conditions, health risks and socio-economic factors. Besides providing for regular updates, AI applications can streamline prevention campaigns, care coordination and holistic chronic disease management, thus saving time and resources.

In addition, AI can be used to predict the effect of prevention campaigns on health outcomes and resource utilization, thus informing decision-makers and optimizing prevention programmes. Such solutions are essential for ensuring improvement in community care by reaching out to many people and aiding in the success of public health initiatives. Data integration, mapping and schema management are fundamental for modern organizations, but they demand considerable time and resources. AI and machine learning (ML) can address this challenge by automating repetitive and labour-intensive tasks. The need for data integration is documented by market and trend analyses that described the AI data integration market as one of the fastest growing one in 2023, with a year-over-year growth rate of 117% (Databriks, 2023).

Products on the market, such as those by IQVIA, a provider of advanced analytics, technology solutions and clinical research services to the life sciences industry, offer solutions managed directly by the supplier, introducing the issue of outsourcing (particularly complex in the public sector) or managed internally by the healthcare companies themselves (Blyton et al., 2023). These products allow users to define complex criteria, analyze patient data and share insights through dashboards and reports, with the advantage of reducing analysis times and the related costs. Some shed light on the clinical characteristics of a treatable population for a specific disease and identify with high precision the doctors who could prescribe treatment, thus optimizing resource use.

Algorithms support the expansion of the diagnosed patient cohort, stimulate growth of the treatable population, identify undiagnosed patients and connect to their treating physicians, thus creating a list of high-potential healthcare targets for personalized or omnichannel campaigns (IQVIA, 2023).

Moreover, to be effective in the community, the choices in population-based medicine need to be supported by patients and the reference community. Also in this case, AI can be decisive for the success of a project's implementation. The involvement of patients and their communities is essential for 'feeding' the AI with updated data. However, this can clash with data use and data integration regulations that may be too stringent for the data to be used to their full potential. Hence, both organizations and governments need to explore how to harness AI to boost innovation and productivity while establishing protective measures to mitigate risks and anticipate the accidents and the mishaps that lie ahead (Blyton et al., 2023).

## HOSPITAL-COMMUNITY INTEGRATION AND NETWORKS

The integration of hospital and community services is a healthcare management approach designed to enhance the consistency and flow of care between hospital facilities and local health services. The goal is to ensure smoother, more efficient and effective delivery of treatment for patients while minimizing a healthcare system's overall costs. In today's challenging economic climate and amidst demographic and epidemiological shifts, organizational models built on integration are crucial for ensuring equal, continuous and uniform access to healthcare services and quality care for all citizens. Operationally, integration can be implemented through a variety of methods, from establishing integrated networks to designing care pathways, and defining intermediary structures between hospitals and local areas, such as the hub-and-spoke model or the pendulum model. The former is an organizational model that centralizes services at a hub to ensure access to advanced care, while peripheral facilities (spokes) provide routine services to local communities. The latter model involves periodic mobility of specialized healthcare staff between facilities. Both models aim to improve efficiency, quality of care and access to healthcare services through sharing resources, knowledge and skills. In this way, AI can play a pivotal role in advancing clinical integration and network development.

Another essential element for refining the integration of healthcare settings is protected discharge. In addition to defining standardized operating protocols, knowing the availability of diaries and beds in the various structures of a network is necessary for optimal planning. While this can happen through shared agendas and documents, AI can play an anticipatory role. Working with the AI Lab Skunkworks team, Kettering General Hospital (UK) has adopted advanced AI solutions to efficiently anticipate and manage patient needs. Although these goals are unrelated to intercompany connections, the project may be well suited to this objective. In fact, the result was a proof-of-concept demonstration through a user interface that offers hospital staff the following capabilities: the ability to view a virtual hospital with updated data on occupancy rates and projected bed demand, the presentation of an advanced allocation model with tips and explanations for the user and testing of the model on a wide range of patients differing in characteristics and associated constraints, in order to validate system performance (Transformation Directorate, 2001). By applying this model to the structures within a network, monitoring of network capabilities and provision of services could be improved.

The two elements crucial for the definition of virtuous integration are the planning and the design of services and facilities. Within this context, AI can improve the supervision of clinical and administrative processes, thus allowing for the rapid updating of multidisciplinary management dashboards. A crucial point is that AI is not and should not be fully autonomous: trained personnel are needed to instruct it. Enhanced control over organizational aspects allows for continual adjustment and improvement, positively impacting the real and the perceived quality of services and performance. The emerging pathways for the development of community activities encompass more than just the restructuring of existing local structures and services; they also involve establishing new connections with hospital settings. Consequently, the management of patients with chronic conditions, currently a major burden on healthcare systems, will play a major role in this context.

## NEW SETTINGS FOR INTERMEDIATE CARE AND NEW 'PRIMARY CARE' FOR COMPLEXITIES

The most comprehensive interpretation of intermediate care is given by the Royal College of Physicians of London, which defines it as *care provided by health services that is outside the resources required by a general hospital but exceeds the capabilities of a primary care team conventional* (Melis et al., 2004). The objective is to strengthen these facilities and bolster their integration with other levels of a healthcare system in order to relieve the pressure on hospitals, while preventing the onset and progression of frailty and functional decline in patients by guaranteeing continuity of care (Sezgin et al., 2020). Innovative intermediate care settings are revolutionizing healthcare by offering personalized solutions for people in need of transitional support, i.e. during transfer between care facilities or to the home.

With the creation of dynamic intermediate care settings and the integration of advanced technologies, the healthcare landscape is evolving towards more responsive, efficient, holistic and compassionate care models. Whether in specialty clinics, community health centres or home-based programmes, the emphasis is on personalized care plans that address not only medical needs but also social and emotional well-being. For AI to be effective in such settings, agencies (e.g. healthcare, public administration, social services, etc.) need to be well integrated with one another. Furthermore, the administrative management of patients during their journey is also important for AI applications.

Wearable devices are both an example and the new frontier of intermediate care. In fact, wearable devices that collect physiological data are becoming seamlessly integrated into people's daily lives in response to the growing need for ambulatory patient monitoring. In addition to cost reduction, disease prevention, and early diagnosis, the devices collect huge amounts of data to feed AI databases for population monitoring. To date, however, few systems are rated Conformité Européene (CE) class II or higher or have US FDA approval. Some support healthcare middleware (Muzny et al., 2020), namely, a set of software that acts as an intermediate between computer structures and programmes, allowing them to communicate despite the differences in protocols and operating systems. This underlines the need to assign them priority on the strategy agenda of healthcare policy makers.

Care models can involve general practitioners (GPs) as gatekeepers that restrict access to secondary care as a means to improve care appropriateness and sustainability. When implemented to enhance community care, AI may also benefit appropriateness for specialist care in hospitals (Buck et al., 2022). To facilitate this, given the number of patients seen every day, there are AI applications that may empty the offices of GPs, thus allowing them to attend to clinically significant cases. An international example is Babylon Health, an application developed and used in the United States but also widely employed elsewhere. It responds to the shortage of GPs through four user interfaces (Symptom Checker, visits with doctors employed by Babylon, Health Check and Monitor) which, thanks to AI applications, monitor the data entered by the patient and suggest actions to be taken more or less promptly. While basic access is free, visits are paid for via a freemium model, with the options of Pay as you go, an annual subscription and a National Health Service (UK NHS) arrangement in some limited areas of the United Kingdom. Freemium, a combination of the words 'free' and 'premium', is a pricing strategy by which a basic product or service is provided for free, while a premium is charged for additional features. Babylon acts as a primary care provider, allowing citizens to access both online and physical visiting services.

## INTERMEDIATE CARE: CLINICAL PATHWAYS

AI can play a key role in monitoring one of the main elements that ensure integration between different settings: clinical pathways (IQVIA, 2023). AI can map the path of one or more patients and their interactions with healthcare workers based on the clinical data of individual patients, the inputs entered by the operators (e.g. timing, care settings and operators involved) and the scientific evidence that AI can retrieve from very large databases. And wearable devices come into play here, too. Thanks to image processing, computer vision, ML and computer graphics, wearables (e.g. Google Glass, Microsoft HoloLens and GoPro) and autonomous mobile devices (e.g. robotic agents) participate in home care by reminding patients to take their medications or, depending on the clinical pathway, prompt them to switch on their device when non-use is detected (Ballocchi, 2020). In this way, treatment compliance is strengthened and health outcomes improved. Moreover, wearable devices may suggest alternatives to certain medications as consistent with personal habits or needs. For example, it can suggest the time for taking medications based on an elderly person's sleep habits in keeping with personal routines and lightning the burden of therapy. Such a personalized approach can boost patient satisfaction without placing undue strain on healthcare personnel.

Furthermore, one of the most complex aspects in the 'human' management of a clinical pathway is how to follow the steps of the pathway itself, which is often repetitive and time-consuming in medical practice. For community care to be effective, efficient and coherent with the principle of appropriateness, patients need to be carefully selected for the care pathway. For instance, Olive Healthcare, a Korean company, employs AI to streamline such diverse processes as eligibility checks, insurance claims, prior authorizations, appointment reminders, billing, data reporting and analytics. Similarly, companies like Apixio and 3M have introduced AI-driven risk adjustment and hierarchical condition category (HCC) auditors to assist healthcare practices in enhancing their coding for quality payment programmes (Lin et al., 2019). These applications can save time, resources and stress for the stakeholders involved in community care. Payment for services and material is relevant because some public healthcare systems do not account for services performed, rendering them non-reimbursable. This results in the underutilization of the potential of these services by organizations or a loss of revenue for virtuous organization that choose to provide them.

## NEW WAYS TO CURE (AND CARE): HOME SETTINGS

Decentralization is becoming a hallmark feature of healthcare systems around the world. Treating people in at home, in their own bed, has a dual (and interconnected) purpose. It relieves the pressure on healthcare facilities and reduces costs, while embracing a holistic vision of care in the comfort of the patient's home.

The role of AI in home care holds promise. One example is sending reminders and monitoring medication intake to reduce medication errors and improve therapy compliance (Vervloet et al., 2012). With the integration of telemedicine and remote telemonitoring systems (e.g. wearable devices) and AI chatbots and virtual nurse assistants, timely interventions can be performed and continuity of care ensured, thus reducing the need for frequent visits and expensive hospital admissions (Ekobena, 2023; Katz, 2023). Furthermore, remote monitoring can cover situations in which a healthcare worker is not immediately available but an AI application can determine that the instance does not require immediate attention. Surveillance, together with clinical predictive capacities, can boost safety and trust in the treatment path of patients and their families.

A monitoring programme created by Vuviy Health operated at the University of Pittsburgh Medical Center (UPMC) uses ML to manage patients with chronic conditions such as heart failure and diabetes after hospital discharge. Patients are provided with a tablet or asked to use their own mobile device to transmit their health information to UPMC. The device monitors the patient's symptoms, blood pressure, weight and oxygen levels while they are at home and contacts their doctor as necessary. The data are analyzed to predict when a patient is at risk of an emergency room visit, so doctors can intervene by phone or via a nurse visit (Johnson, 2023).

Certain companies employ 4D imaging alongside sensors and algorithms to identify unusual behaviour patterns and detect alterations in movement. This prompts notification to caregivers or medical workers and facilitates swift intervention to prevent or address falls. From an administrative and a management perspective, this is fundamental: AI applications can help healthcare companies rationalize resources by programming treatment in a patient's home with the aid of a medical worker only as needed. Furthermore, based on clinical findings, predictions can be made about a patient's future needs for which AI applications will be able to programme higher care levels and determine the level of support staff needed for primary care practices (e.g. physician assistants, nurse practitioners, advanced practice providers, clinical pharmacists and social workers) (Lin et al., 2019).

The need for new professional figures and training of staff in new technologies will be addressed in the next chapter.

## REFERENCES

Alowais, S. A., Alghamdi, S. S., Alsuhebany, N., Alqahtani, T., Alshaya, A. I., Almohareb, S. N., Aldairem, A., Alrashed, M., Bin Saleh, K., Badreldin, H. A., Al Yami, M. S., Al Harbi, S., & Albekairy, A. M. (2023). Revolutionizing healthcare: The role of artificial intelligence in clinical practice. *BMC Medical Education*, *23*(1), 689. https://doi.org/10.1186/s12909-023-04698-z

Ballocchi, A. (2020, September 21). Intelligenza artificiale e wearable device per gli ambienti di vita e la fabbrica del futuro. *Tech4Future*. https://tech4future.info/intelligenza-artificiale-wearable-device-applicazioni/

Blyton, A., Carbin, M., O'Connell, O., Rzonca, N., Schaefer, R. S., Stoddard, C., & Zaharia, M. (2023). *The great acceleration: CIO perspectives on generative AI*. https://www.databricks.com/resources/ebook/mit-cio-generative-ai-report?utm_source=mit&utm_medium=display&utm_campaign=7018y000001fhxlqa0

Buck, C., Doctor, E., Hennrich, J., Jöhnk, J., & Eymann, T. (2022). General practitioners' attitudes toward artificial intelligence–enabled systems: Interview study. *Journal of Medical Internet Research*, *24*(1), e28916. https://doi.org/10.2196/28916

Databriks. (2023). *2023 State of Data + AI Powered by the Databricks Lakehouse*. https://www.databricks.com/discover/state-of-data-ai

Ekobena, J. (2023, August 28). AI vs. The human touch: What the new technology means for home care businesses. *Forbs*. https://www.forbes.com/sites/forbesbusinesscouncil/2023/08/28/ai-vs-the-human-touch-what-the-new-technology-means-for-home-care-businesses/?sh=48530ed85146

IQVIA. (2023). *Elevate your brand growth*. IQVIA. https://www.iqvia.com/solutions/real-world-evidence/health-data-apps-and-ai/commercial-and-brand-patient-profiling?utm_medium=cpc&utm_source=google&utm_campaign=2024_gadsNewPagesX_DTAAI_RS&utm_term=clinical%20data%20integration&utm_content=157265885234#P

Johnson, S. R. (2023). *The future is now? AI's role in healthcare starts small, gets bigger*. Modern Helathcare in Depth.

Katz, S. (2023, April 11). *How UPMC is bringing AI into patient care. Inside life changing medicine*. University of Pittsburg. https://inside.upmc.com/how-upmc-is-bringing-ai-into-patient-care/

Lin, S. Y., Mahoney, M. R., & Sinsky, C. A. (2019). Ten ways artificial intelligence will transform primary care. *Journal of General Internal Medicine*, *34*(8), 1626–1630. https://doi.org/10.1007/s11606-019-05035-1

Melis, R. J. F., Rikkert, M. G. M. O., Parker, S. G., & van Eijken, M. I. J. (2004). What is intermediate care? *BMJ*, *329*(7462), 360–361. https://doi.org/10.1136/bmj.329.7462.360

Mittelstadt, B. (2022). *The impact of artificial intelligence on the doctor-patient relationship*. https://www.coe.int/en/web/bioethics/report-impact-of-ai-on-the-doctor-patient-relationship

Muzny, M., Henriksen, A., Giordanengo, A., Muzik, J., Grøttland, A., Blixgård, H., Hartvigsen, G., & Årsand, E. (2020). Wearable sensors with possibilities for data exchange: Analyzing status and needs of different actors in mobile health monitoring systems. *International Journal of Medical Informatics*, *133*, 104017. https://doi.org/10.1016/j.ijmedinf.2019.104017

Sezgin, D., O'Caoimh, R., Liew, A., O'Donovan, M. R., Illario, M., Salem, M. A., Kennelly, S., Carriazo, A. M., Lopez-Samaniego, L., Carda, C. A., Rodriguez-Acuña, R., Inzitari, M., Hammar, T., & Hendry, A. (2020). The effectiveness of intermediate care including transitional care interventions on function, healthcare utilisation and costs: A scoping review. *European Geriatric Medicine*, *11*(6), 961–974. https://doi.org/10.1007/s41999-020-00365-4

Transformation Directorate. (2001, December 10). *Improving hospital bed allocation using AI*. NHS England. https://transform.england.nhs.uk/ai-lab/explore-all-resources/topic/design-and-build-ai/

Vervloet, M., Linn, A. J., van Weert, J. C. M., de Bakker, D. H., Bouvy, M. L., & van Dijk, L. (2012). The effectiveness of interventions using electronic reminders to improve adherence to chronic medication: A systematic review of the literature. *Journal of the American Medical Informatics Association*, *19*(5), 696–704. https://doi.org/10.1136/amiajnl-2011-000748

# 4

# KEY EMERGING AI DEVELOPMENTS IN HEALTHCARE


## ABSTRACT

Common challenges for healthcare systems worldwide are population ageing, rising therapy spending and reduced economic resources. In response, AI can play a crucial role in facilitating managerial and economic objectives within a holistic vision of care and improve the experience of patients and professionals. AI may change the delivery of services and the demand for them as well. This raises questions of how to balance the supply and demand sides of healthcare services, how to leverage competitive positioning and how to differentiate strategies specific to the public and to the private sector.



**Keywords**: Artificial intelligence; healthcare demand; healthcare supply; healthcare sector issues; innovative solutions; return on investment; competitive levers


Clinical and management issues often clash, creating situations in which physicians and managers are hard pressed to resolve the sources of conflict. AI can aid decision-makers in better understanding the link between problems and opportunities and how to find innovative solutions. Health systems around the world share several common challenges: increased chronicity in ageing populations, rising costs of novel therapies and limitations in human and economic resources.

## CHALLENGES FOR HEALTHCARE SYSTEMS

### Demographics Impacts

People are living longer but with the risk of living longer with a chronic condition. This places an enormous burden on healthcare systems. The ageing population has trouble accessing care yet has the need for increasingly expensive care in the course of treatment (Chen et al., 2023; Pickett & Wilkinson, 2015). Furthermore, while some public health systems can provide patients with free or nearly treatment, the economic resources for accessing treatment are becoming increasingly scarce (Lynch et al., 2004).

The causes for population ageing are lower birth rates and longer life expectancy. The latter is largely influenced by new technologies for managing diseases which were once considered incurable and by more effective treatment of chronic conditions. Advances in technology have a positive effect on human progress in general and on the quality of life, now largely taken for granted.

Patients who are better informed about what is happening around them will demand more and better care: awareness about personal health and healthy behaviour has grown partly, thanks to the Internet, whereas health literacy has not kept pace (Keene Woods et al., 2023; NIHR, 2022). There is also the risk of information overload, which may confuse patients seeking medical attention (Liu & Jiang, 2024). For healthcare systems, management needs to focus its efforts on professional updating of personnel, infrastructures and technologies. Knowledge especially in this field is advancing at an ever-increasing rate as novel technologies, together with the knowledge they are based on, appear on the market. Similarly, diagnostic and therapeutic pathways are regularly updated to achieve better care delivery (OECD, 2019). What a professional did a year ago might now be obsolete, even potentially dangerous for a patient; the consequence of this ongoing advancement is the constant need to stay updated to provide the best possible service for patients. But access to information, especially accurate information, takes time and time, is exactly what healthcare workers often lack.

## Workforce Challenges

Complexities and difficulties can be experienced by patients and professionals working in the clinical and the administrative sides of healthcare. Although working in a contest that should be well organized, healthcare professionals often experience burnout, which affects their lives and those of their patients, too. Burnout among healthcare workers is underestimated in both number and importance. The COVID-19 pandemic exacerbated the phenomenon and accelerated workforce turnover. It is estimated that over half of healthcare workers are affected (De Hert, 2020; Rotenstein et al., 2023; Willard-Grace et al., 2019).

According to the World Health Organization (WHO), burnout refers to a syndrome resulting from chronic workplace stress that has not been successfully managed. It is characterized by feelings of exhaustion, increased distance from work and a reduction in professional efficacy (WHO, 2019). This means that mental and physical stress has increased due to longer work periods and later retirement age, impacting the health of individuals in advanced age. The main risk factors for burnout in healthcare workers are young age, high-risk procedures and the absence of a work–life balance (Lacy & Chan, 2018).

The ability to tackle this enormous complexity by modifying the context in which healthcare professionals work is key to improving health and well-being. When healthcare professionals work in an environment aligned with their ideals, they are better able to provide care to the best of their abilities.

The current situation is one of economic hardship and lack of personnel. The projected healthcare personnel shortages raise concern about the future, particularly in the United States, where the healthcare workforce will lose 195,400 nurses by 2031 and up to 124,000 physicians over the next 12 years but gain an expected 37% in openings for home health aides and personal health aides by 2028 (O'Connell-Domenech, 2023). The data for Europe are similarly bleak (WHO, 2023). The strategic directors of healthcare companies find it increasingly difficult to innovate and keep up with new developments while maintaining acceptable standards of care.

## Other impacts on Health System performance

The characteristics and specificities of healthcare have implications for the structure and dynamics of the systems themselves. For instance, waiting lists are growing longer (Amigoni et al., 2023). Limited funding and resources granted to health systems have led to a shortage of health workers, facilities and equipment, resulting in dissatisfaction with services. To prevent this from generating longer waiting lists, political and healthcare decision-makers will have to question current operational and governance models. As seen in the previous chapters, AI can play a crucial role by making the current production system more efficient with investments in technology and training. Furthermore, AI allows for greater decentralization of decisions and data collection, together with centralized monitoring to coordinate staff and facilities efficiently and effectively.

Moreover, while the growth of the private sector may be a cause for concern, it has become an increasingly attractive alternative to the public sector for both patients and employees (Independent Healthcare Provider Networks, 2022). Furthermore, in healthcare systems where private companies offer their services like a public service through accreditation with the NHS, as in Italy, the public sector should exploit these synergies to improve its own services. Also here AI can make the public sector more efficient by planning requests for coverage by accredited private sector operators and more accurate monitoring of the latter.

Against this background, new paradigms should also be examined to understand the full potential of AI in improving – or even just simplifying – a health system's performance. In particular, the reorganization of services around the patient with a view to holistic management of their needs involves the search for a balance between standardization of care and personalization of treatment. One example is the decentralization of care from the hospital to the community, as described in Chapter 3. A quick overview of these impacts is displayed in Fig. 8.

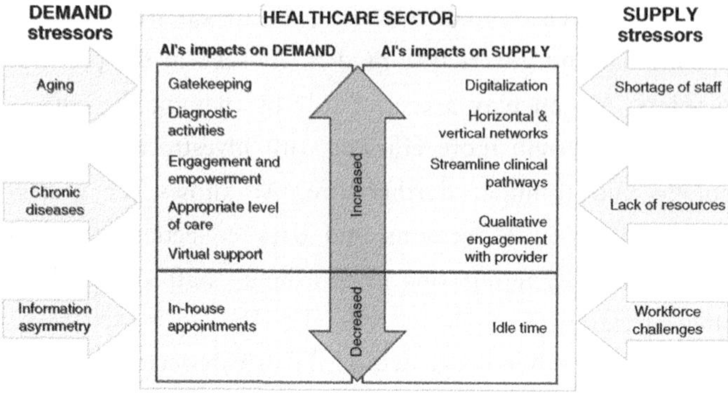


*Source:* The authors.

**Fig. 8. The Impact of AI on the Challenges Facing Healthcare Systems.**

## ARTIFICIAL INTELLIGENCE (AI): A PROBLEM-SOLVING TOOL

In 2023, Forbes described AI as a 'prosthesis for the brain' (McKendrick, 2023). The global impact of AI on healthcare is hard to estimate quantitatively, whether positively or negatively, because of the numerous variables involved in each application. Its qualitative impact on processes can be explored, however. The two key dimensions are: the ability to control healthcare demand and supply independent of each other.

### Impact on Healthcare Demand: AI Gatekeepers

People seeking medical attention can now 'download your physician'. Many companies (e.g. Babylon Health, Health Tap, Ada, Buoy and Your.MD) have developed 'AI doctors' who provide, with a diagnostic accuracy comparable to that of human doctors, health advice directly to patients with common symptoms, thus freeing up access to primary care for more complex care (Mukherjee, 2017). This does not mean, however, that health professionals are no longer needed, but rather what has changed is the way that they are used. A major differentiation from the human-based model of seeking medical attention will take place through second visits and requests for specialist services.

In cases of diagnostic complexity, patients may be referred to the wrong healthcare professional or undergo a lengthy process before a definitive diagnosis can be made (Ali et al., 2023). This means a waste of time for both the patient and the professional. AI can help to circumscribe the doubts about a specific condition, reducing the probability of encountering the wrong healthcare specialist and lengthening the pathway of management and care. This could lead to an increased demand for diagnostic services and second opinions from human primary care physicians.

From an operational perspective, institutions need to operate synergistically within a healthcare system to regulate the use of these platforms and ensure equality and equity in the gatekeeping function of general practitioners (GPs). This needs to be maintained and supported by AI applications to improve the inter-diagnostic patient journey. To this end, clinical path design should build in AI applications (integrating administrative and clinical AI). For example, AI can be included in clinical pathways for use in diagnosis and in the post-discharge period (e.g. home care and follow-up) and in treatment monitoring. Furthermore, the formalization of a systemic use of AI to improve health outcomes and the cost-effectiveness of chronic care will allow directors to formalize the managerial aspects that revolve around AI: personnel, training, economic resources and techniques.

Thus, AI will accelerate the task of shifting, which will be discussed in the following paragraphs.

By altering healthcare consumption habits, AI can achieve a dual purpose: reduce inappropriate diagnostic services and demands on primary care physicians. In so doing, this effect can trickle down to reduce inappropriate secondary-level services, thus shortening waiting lists.

## Impact on Healthcare Supply

For the system's response to be appropriate and coherent with the demand for healthcare needs, it is important to continuously renew the methods of providing services. AI plays a crucial role in this too. However, the implementation methods are even more specific than individual projects for certain clinical conditions or for certain administrative tasks. For AI to be able to change how services are provided, without creating inequity of access, healthcare decision-makers need to implement the algorithms uniformly throughout the organization. Furthermore, AI should be systematically implemented, without stopping at the 'grounding' of the incorporation project.

Clinical pathways are amenable to this approach. Indeed, clinical pathways allow for multidisciplinary integration, facilitate the transparent satisfaction of patient needs by providing concise documentation to healthcare personnel on the services to be provided and determine the resources necessary for patient care (Asmirajanti et al., 2018). Moreover, they are also a good ally for clinical leaders and healthcare managers for structuring horizontal and vertical clinical networks in administrative and clinical applications.

Horizontal networks are characterized by multiple complex specialist centres (hubs) and numerous spoke centres throughout a catchment area. AI can work according to a hub and spoke network model, collecting data from various sources and then aggregating them into a single output. As mentioned in the previous chapter on community integration, administrative AI applications aid in resource monitoring and allocation. Differently, clinical AI applications ensure that all network operators have updated, integrated data and monitor patient status. In brief, AI can facilitate a holistic approach to patients with chronic conditions by improving the integration between specialists and the outcomes for treating concomitant conditions.

Vertical networks are characterized by relationships between levels of assistance in which the response to health needs is based on complexity and severity: from primary or home care to highly specialized hospital care. AI plays a dual role: administrative applications are used to streamline admission and transfer processes while clinical applications are employed in the analysis of a patient's clinical data and for referral to the appropriate network level.

From the perspective of service provision, fundamental factors are dematerialization of the networks themselves and the integration of protectionists. Patients with low care complexity will no longer need to move from one network to another (horizontal or vertical) but rather can be monitored remotely via virtual assistants, intelligent rooms and wearable devices among other means. With AI applications, the patient's home will become a place of care integrated into the care networks where patients are their own case manager. In this way, intervention by healthcare workers with patients at the network sites will be limited to situations of necessity and appropriateness. The same approach for both administrative and non-administrative AI applications can be used in hub & spokes network models for diagnostic services and follow-up.

Diagnostics are being conducted more and more via points of care, i.e. places where clinical laboratory tests are performed (pharmacy, doctor's office, clinic, community centre or home). Point-of-care (POC) diagnostics, such as those based on microfluidic and lab-on-a-chip (LOC) technologies, can provide test results within minutes, thus enabling timely treatment decisions and minimizing patient anxiety (McRae et al., 2022). These operational solutions constitute an improvement in the provision of services, but AI can boost their efficiency, making them not only a logistic factor but also a quality factor in the use of a service (10.3343/alm.2023.43.5.401), while reducing the workload on hub laboratories. In fact, smart diagnostics, i.e. in vitro diagnostics that exploit the power of AI, bring prevention and monitoring closer to the patient and personalize therapies with a single test. For example, the Cardiac ScoreCard hardware developed by the McDevitt laboratory is a universal multiplex cardiac biomarker test combined with clinical decision support tools that provide diagnostic and prognostic information on a spectrum of cardiovascular diseases, including cardiac health, acute myocardial infarction and heart failure (Khan et al., 2023).

Moreover, the integration of administrative and non-administrative (clinical) AI applications into the workflow of healthcare professionals deserves further exploration due to its impact on their work and personal lives. It has been estimated that about 40% of a professional's tasks is automatable (Manyika et al., 2017), meaning that roughly half of working time is devoted to activities that have little to do with the profession, such as documenting medical procedures or repetitive tasks that do not require special skills. A major reduction in this 'out-of-focus' time will allow professionals to direct their attention to the patient, improving the experience and the health outcome in many cases, as well. Furthermore, this will allow better communication with patients, thus reducing the risk of misunderstanding, while improving adherence to therapies and clinical pathways.

Furthermore, AI can play a meaningful role in direct communication with patients, increasing their engagement and empowerment along their journey. In addition to providing constant feedback to healthcare personnel on their communication skills to understand whether they are effective in achieving patient satisfaction (Butow & Hoque, 2020), AI software connected to wearable devices allows for timely prompts and reminders, as well as direct contact with the healthcare sector via chatbots, making healthcare communication more engaging, relevant, exciting and actionable (Kreps & Neuhauser, 2013; Siala & Wang, 2022).

Another substantial change in the offer is undoubtedly the acceleration of task shifting and skill mixing in healthcare. A key role will be played by GPs, who should not be left alone to meet the challenge of managing chronic patients (Lega, 2023). However, given the critical lack of staff and the need to increase gatekeeping by GPs, it is important that they are supported also remotely by specialists. AI's prediction and diagnostic capabilities can support GPs in gatekeeping, since its data validation and aggregation opportunities allow for better communication with higher levels of care without 'moving' the patient. In addition, health and social workers will see their work modified by AI and the provision of their services as a consequence. Interventions at patients' homes can be much better targeted with advanced remote monitoring and treatment decisions made on site can be more prudent based on the entire clinical picture, a patient's socio-economic status and prognosis.

Nevertheless, the key emphasis lies not in necessarily assigning these tasks to AI, but rather in the potential of AI, with its inherent characteristics, to accelerate the underlying processes causing a slowdown in hospital activities. Accelerating processes entails not only executing them more swiftly but also restructuring them to eliminate superfluous and unnecessarily prolonged steps, favouring a more streamlined mode of operation. As highlighted in Chapter 1, AI can identify and optimize redundant steps, thus reshaping the entire workflow. Once a task is delegated to AI, it has the potential to enhance efficiency and reduce unnecessary time wasted.

## WHY HEALTHCARE MANAGERS SHOULD LOOK AHEAD TO CREATE VALUE

It is challenging to say how much more sustainable an AI-based system is compared to the current state of healthcare. Yet qualitative and quantitative estimations are possible. Until now, the discussion has focused on the effectiveness and efficiency of AI in healthcare, but in an environment with scarce resources, the return on investment (ROI) is decisive for the choice. ROI is divided into hard, based on the standard definition of the financial relationship between the gain or loss of an investment compared to its cost, and soft, which also takes into account various levers of competitive advantage such as employee satisfaction and loyalty, skills acquisition, improved branding and a higher valuation of the company or organization (Rao, 2021). A good manager must take both aspects into account.

For AI, hard ROI derives from various factors:

- Time savings (and costs) simplifying repetitive manual and cognitive tasks, thus reducing processing times, such as forecasting, billing or reporting.

- Productivity increment directly related to the growth in the decision-making capacity of AI (the more data it is fed, the more accurate its outputs will be).
- Revenue growth achieved through AI-enhanced services that offer new value propositions.

To these can be added soft returns in the organization's image and reputation and enabling critical success factors, such as:

- An organization's ability to predict and address emerging challenges more promptly than in the past.
- Enhanced patient experience thanks to personalized service.
- Patient loyalty through the creation of digital networks and the dematerialization of information.

Indeed, in addition to the greater demand for health per se and the way in which services are delivered, AI is also reshuffling the factors that can generate competitive advantages for healthcare companies. There are several competitive success factors that AI can influence and with which healthcare organizations can work to achieve high patient satisfaction. Numerous factors have been mentioned above (creation of networks, dedicated fast tracks and systematized follow-up), also minimizing the time health services take to complete plays a major role: pre-admission, the procedure itself and post-discharge.

Furthermore, people are asking for a progressive dematerialization of activities. Thanks to AI, mainly but not only administrative tasks, it will be possible to reduce many steps in direct contact with a healthcare centre. The same applies to the insurance sector, which is growing steadily with the national health system. Moreover, dematerialization and innovative technologies have a strong impact on the patient experience and on the work of operators.

Finally, AI can play a key role in defining the service formula based on detailed target segmentation and implementation of an organization's performance management capabilities.

To conclude, it is important to remember how relevant storytelling is to stakeholders. Having a strong brand identity need not be the prerogative of a private sector which benefits from an often greater availability of resources. Thanks to AI, the public health sector can also become the cutting edge for young population segments who should be viewed as future service users and as current 'not yet patients' to be reached with health prevention programmes.

AI applications can be fit to single organizations and to systems. However, the healthcare system may also benefit from another opportunity regarding payment methods. Bundled payments, for example, where the reimbursed sum is fixed and divided among the providers who have cared for the patient. This avoids paying for individual services, tests and procedures and seeks to align the interests of providers in improving the effectiveness and efficiency of the multidisciplinary team in relation to the patient. This type of payment is widely used with diagnosis related groups (DRGs) by hospitals, but several healthcare systems have also implemented it at the community and home care level for post-acute treatment and long-term care. Debate surrounds the economic advantages of this payment method, due to the difficulty in predicting potential complications during hospital stay, which are not anticipated in the formulation of DRGs, as well as managing the natural heterogeneity of patients and risk stratification (Agarwal et al., 2020; Lino et al., 2023; Shih et al., 2015). Nonetheless, the predictive capabilities of AI can overcome this obstacle. Furthermore, the implementation of bundled payments at the community level is hindered by the inability to manage data external to the hospital. The public sector struggles to attain the level of detailed data required for this type of financing. Unlike the insurance sector, which can track a patient's entire therapeutic journey through billing, the public sector only accounts for individual services performed. AI applications could aid in the management of a vast amount of data and correlate it autonomously, and therefore anonymously for the operators, thereby providing a summary of the patient's entire care journey and allowing for strong hospital–community integration.

In summary, a healthcare supply chain that uses AI can effectively streamline the workflow for all stakeholders involved. Obviously, for this to happen AI applications need to be well integrated and designed as an extension of human possibilities – not a world in which human beings live to work, but rather a world in which they work to live and where the expectations of patients and operators can be aligned with the delivery capabilities of the health system itself. The next chapter discusses the strategies that a good decision-maker will want to employ when introducing AI into a healthcare organization.

## REFERENCES

Agarwal, R., Liao, J. M., Gupta, A., & Navathe, A. S. (2020). The impact of bundled payment on health care spending, utilization, and quality: A systematic review. *Health Affairs*, *39*(1), 50–57. https://doi.org/10.1377/hlthaff.2019.00784

Ali, O., Abdelbaki, W., Shrestha, A., Elbasi, E., Alryalat, M. A. A., & Dwivedi, Y. K. (2023). A systematic literature review of artificial intelligence in the healthcare sector: Benefits, challenges, methodologies, and functionalities. *Journal of*

*Innovation & Knowledge*, *8*(1), 100333. https://doi.org/10.1016/j.jik.2023.100333

Amigoni, F., Lega, F., & Maggioni, E. (2023). Insights into how universal, tax-funded, single payer health systems manage their waiting lists: A review of the literature. *Health Services Management Research*. https://doi.org/10.1177/09514848231186773

Asmirajanti, M., Syuhaimie Hamid, A. Y., & Hariyati, T. S. (2018). Clinical care pathway strenghens interprofessional collaboration and quality of health service: A literature review. *Enfermería Clínica*, *28*, 240–244. https://doi.org/10.1016/S1130-8621(18)30076-7

Butow, P., & Hoque, E. (2020). Using artificial intelligence to analyse and teach communication in healthcare. *The Breast*, *50*, 49–55. https://doi.org/10.1016/j.breast.2020.01.008

Chen, J., Zhao, M., Zhou, R., Ou, W., & Yao, P. (2023). How heavy is the medical expense burden among the older adults and what are the contributing factors? A literature review and problem-based analysis. *Frontiers in Public Health*, *11*. https://doi.org/10.3389/fpubh.2023.1165381

De Hert, S. (2020). Burnout in healthcare workers: Prevalence, impact and preventative strategies. *Local and Regional Anesthesia*, *13*, 171–183. https://doi.org/10.2147/LRA.S240564

Independent Healthcare Providers Networks. (2022, December 5). Private healthcare providers expect growth in all key markets in coming year as demand for care soars. *Independent Healthcare Providers Networks*. https://www.ihpn.org.uk/news/private-healthcare-providers-expect-growth-in-all-key-markets-in-coming-year-as-demand-for-care-soars/

Keene Woods, N., Ali, U., Medina, M., Reyes, J., & Chesser, A. K. (2023). Health literacy, health outcomes and equity: A trend analysis based on a population survey. *Journal of Primary Care & Community Health*, *14*. https://doi.org/10.1177/21501319231156132

Khan, A. I., Khan, M., & Khan, R. (2023). Artificial intelligence in point-of-care testing. *Annals of Laboratory Medicine*, *43*(5), 401–407. https://doi.org/10.3343/alm.2023.43.5.401

Kreps, G. L., & Neuhauser, L. (2013). Artificial intelligence and immediacy: Designing health communication to personally engage consumers and providers. *Patient Education and Counseling*, *92*(2), 205–210. https://doi.org/10.1016/j.pec.2013.04.014

Lacy, B. E., & Chan, J. L. (2018). Physician burnout: The hidden health care crisis. *Clinical Gastroenterology and Hepatology*, *16*(3), 311–317. https://doi.org/10.1016/j.cgh.2017.06.043

Lega, F. (2023). Cure primarie e servizi territoriali. In *Economia e Management sanitario* (3rd ed., pp. 261–263). Egea.

Lino, A. D. A. D. S., Cruz, J. A. S. D., Porto, B. C., Nogueira, R. P., Otoch, J. P., & Artifon, E. L. D. A. (2023). Comparing financing models for supplementary healthcare in appendectomy: Activity-based costing (fee-for-service) vs. diagnosis related group remuneration (bundled payment) – A systematic review and meta-analysis. *Acta Cirúrgica Brasileira*, *38*. https://doi.org/10.1590/acb386923

Liu, J., & Jiang, H. (2024). Exploring the effects of online physician voice pitch range and filled pauses on patient satisfaction in mobile health communication. *Health*

*Communication*, 1–14. https://doi.org/10.1080/10410236.2024.2313791

Lynch, J., Smith, G. D., Harper, S., Hillemeier, M., Ross, N., Kaplan, G. A., & Wolfson, M. (2004). Is income inequality a determinant of population health? Part 1. A systematic review. *The Milbank Quarterly*, *82*(1), 5–99. https://doi.org/10.1111/j.0887-378X.2004.00302.x

Manyika, J., Lund, S., Chui, M., Bughin, J., Woetzel, J., Batra, P., Ko, R., & Sanghvi, S. (2017). *Jobs lost, jobs gained: Workforce transitions in a time of automation*. https://www.mckinsey.com/~/media/mckinsey/industries/public%20and%20social%20sector/our%20insights/what%20the%20future%20of%20work%20will%20mean%20for%20jobs%20skills%20and%20wages/mgi-jobs-lost-jobs-gained-executive-summary-december-6-2017.pdf

McKendrick, J. (2023, May 24). How generative AI could give us back at least 40% of our time. *Forbes*. https://www.forbes.com/sites/joemckendrick/2023/05/24/how-generative-ai-could-give-us-back-at-least-40-of-our-time/?sh=236b9a032efc

McRae, M. P., Rajsri, K. S., Alcorn, T. M., & McDevitt, J. T. (2022). Smart diagnostics: Combining artificial intelligence and in vitro diagnostics. *Sensors*, 22(17), 6355. https://doi.org/10.3390/s22176355

Mukherjee, S. (2017, January 10). You can now download an artificial intelligence doctor. *Fortune*. https://fortune.com/2017/01/10/healthtap-dr-ai-launch/

NIHR. (2022). Health information: Are you getting your message across? https://doi.org/10.3310/nihrevidence_51109

O'Connell-Domenech, A. (2023, September 28). *The US is suffering a healthcare worker shortage. Experts fear it will only get worse*. Changing America. https://thehill.com/changing-america/well-being/prevention-cures/4225960-the-us-is-suffering-a-healthcare-worker-shortage-experts-fear-it-will-only-get-worse/

OECD. (2019). *Improving healthcare quality in Europe* (R. Busse, N. Klazinga, D. Panteli, & W. Quentin, Eds.; Health Policy Series, Vol. 53). European Observatory on Health Systems and Policies.

Pickett, K. E., & Wilkinson, R. G. (2015). Income inequality and health: A causal review. *Social Science & Medicine*, *128*, 316–326. https://doi.org/10.1016/j.socscimed.2014.12.031

Rao, A. (2021, June 20). *Solving AI's ROI problem. It's not that easy*. PWC.

Rotenstein, L. S., Brown, R., Sinsky, C., & Linzer, M. (2023). The association of work overload with burnout and intent to leave the job across the healthcare workforce during COVID-19. *Journal of General Internal Medicine*, *38*(8), 1920–1927. https://doi.org/10.1007/s11606-023-08153-z

Shih, T., Chen, L. M., & Nallamothu, B. K. (2015). Will bundled payments change health care? Examining the evidence thus far in cardiovascular care. *Circulation*, *131*(24), 2151–2158. https://doi.org/10.1161/CIRCULATIONAHA.114.010393

Siala, H., & Wang, Y. (2022). SHIFTing artificial intelligence to be responsible in healthcare: A systematic review. *Social Science & Medicine*, *296*, 114782. https://doi.org/10.1016/j.socscimed.2022.114782

WHO. (2023). *Newly adopted Declaration spells out how political action can protect, support and invest in health workers across Europe and central Asia*. https://www.who.int/europe/news/item/22-03-2023-the-health-workforce-crisis-in-europe-is-no-longer-a-looming-threat—it-is-here-and-now.-the-bucharest-declaration-charts-a-way-forward

WHO. (2019, May 28). *Burn-out an "occupational phenomenon": International classification of diseases*. World Health Organization. https://www.who.int/news/item/28-05-2019-burn-out-an-occupational-phenomenon-international-classification-of-diseases

Willard-Grace, R., Knox, M., Huang, B., Hammer, H., Kivlahan, C., & Grumbach, K. (2019). Burnout and health care workforce turnover. *The Annals of Family Medicine*, *17*(1), 36–41. https://doi.org/10.1370/afm.2338

# 5

# A GUIDE TO IMPLEMENTING AI IN THE WORKFLOW


## ABSTRACT

Several primary challenges can be identified in the strategic application of AI for organizational optimization within the operational framework of diverse healthcare settings. To develop future clinical leaders, essential skills and competencies need to be cultivated within teams through training and support. The overarching aims are to foster skills for health management and leadership, as well as promote organizational behaviour for change and health system facilitators (i.e. payment systems and health information systems) to incentivize adoption. This chapter provides readers with a comprehensive roadmap for the implementation of AI in healthcare settings.



**Keywords**: Implementation; performance indicators; development; training; leadership; roadmap; framework; organizational behaviour; organizational readiness

The implementation of AI-driven software can be fraught with challenges. Notable hurdles include resistance to change and apprehension about inherent biases against AI technologies, the most common of which is the fear of job displacement. This makes collaborative effort crucial in the co-creation between healthcare providers and technology companies to ensure trust, promote adoption and ultimately implement AI as a tool for advancing healthcare and management. This chapter addresses various factors in planning a successful approach with a roadmap to implementing AI.

## ORGANIZATIONAL READINESS

The thoughtful implementation of AI into healthcare systems takes into account organizational culture and the external regulatory and financial environment within which a healthcare organization operates. Leadership characterized by transformational qualities (e.g. the cultivation of involvement, commitment and teamwork) has the potential to nurture a positive organizational culture. According to a paper coauthored by Curt Langlotz, director of the Stanford Centre for AI in Medicine and Imaging, alignment with organizational goals is key to organizational readiness for data sharing for the implementation of AI (Youssef et al., 2023). Moreover, the authors report that organizational champions were pivotal in initiating and promoting data sharing efforts (Youssef et al., 2023). Indeed, the organizational qualities of professionals are essential. This topic will be further discussed in the section on leadership and organizational behaviour.

## NEW POSITIONS AND TRAINING

According to research by the Boston Consulting Group, 9 out of 10 CEOs rank AI as a top priority, but only 1 out of 10 leading companies have trained more than one-quarter of their employees on GenAI tools (Lesser & Schweizer, 2024). This misalignment warrants the attention of healthcare companies. Indeed, healthcare organizations need to raise the digital literacy of their workforce to a fairly detailed understanding of AI. It is also in the interest of professionals to stay informed through learning, development and willingness to change (NHS, 2019). Furthermore, the era of AI brings new roles into an organization. Clinical leaders should consider the creation of positions in teams responsible for the implementation of AI within their organization, such as data scientists, data engineers and a chief AI officer (CAIO).

The roles are specific to the particular needs of a given healthcare organization, since organizational structures and job roles can and will evolve. There are several key figures a general healthcare organization can consider when implementing AI solutions. Key figures in data management include data experts, staff tasked with data entry, its management and quality, as well as building datasets. Data scientists analyze large datasets, apply machine learning algorithms to identify patterns and trends, develop predictive models, and draw relevant insights from the data. Data engineers design, build and maintain the infrastructure necessary to support AI and machine learning applications; they collaborate with the data scientists to ensure seamless integration of algorithms into other systems and applications. Data managers, scientists and engineers work closely together to build datasets and infrastructures to gain valuable insights via AI applications. AI engineers develop and optimize AI algorithms and work very closely with the data engineers. The overall strategy and implementation of AI initiatives are typically overseen by a CAIO. The CAIO, in turn, collaborates closely with AI

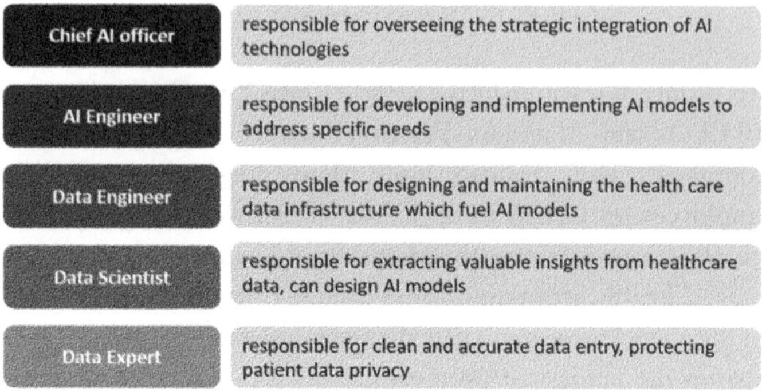


*Source:* The authors.

**Fig. 9. Examples of New Professional Roles Related to AI in Healthcare Organizations.**

engineers, data engineers, scientists and executives as well. Since different healthcare organizations have different needs, other roles or variations of those mentioned above can be considered (see Fig. 9).

## A ROAD MAP FOR IMPLEMENTING AI

The successful implementation of AI proceeds through general phases. The roadmap is a plan to achieve a successful launch of meaningful AI for organizational optimization in a healthcare setting. This simplified framework starts with a preparatory phase, followed by a tool development phase and a launch phase. The duration of each phase is context-specific for a given healthcare setting (team size, organization size, etc.). A systematic approach to AI implementation will aid healthcare managers through the phases of adoption and integration of AI technologies in their organization, while prioritizing patient care and regulatory compliance (see Fig. 10).

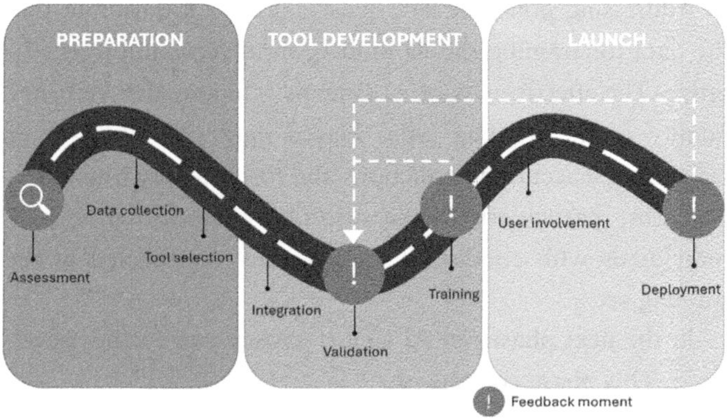


*Source:* The authors.

**Fig. 10. Road map for AI Implementation.**

The preparatory phase is exploratory and entails:

- Assessment: Assess the current processes within a healthcare organization and pinpoint areas where AI can add value (e.g. diagnostics, patient management and general administration). Define the objectives of the AI solution precisely, i.e. whether the focus is on enhancing efficiency, patient outcomes or reducing costs. Also ensure alignment of these goals with the organization's overarching healthcare strategy.
- Data collection: Gather relevant high-quality healthcare data compliant with privacy regulations and legislation. Robust datasets are crucial for AI models to provide precise and reliable insights.
- Tool selection: Select AI tools or platforms that align with the specific healthcare context based on factors such as machine learning algorithms, natural language processing or computer vision, depending on the application.

Addressing potential data bias is central to ensuring that the data for training the AI models are diverse and representative. The effectiveness of AI systems is inherently tied to the quality of the training data. Biased data pose the risk of generating inaccurate predictions and fostering discriminatory practices, particularly those affecting minority groups or individuals with conditions inadequately represented in the training set.

In the next phase, an AI tool is chosen and further developed. This phase consists of:

- Integration: Ensure smooth integration with current healthcare software in place. The key to success is compatibility, as it allows AI to enhance existing workflows without causing disruption.
- Validation: Involve healthcare professionals to validate AI models in clinical settings. This step ensures that the technology aligns with medical standards and practise. Verify adherence to healthcare regulations and standards to protect patient privacy and data security.
- Training: Train the AI models with the collected data. Ongoing refinement and validation are essential to ensure adherence to regulatory and clinical realities, as well as to adapt to evolving healthcare scenarios.

After tool development, the organization and the tool are ready for the launch phase:

- User involvement: Provide training for healthcare staff to effectively use AI tools. Garner acceptance and support from stakeholders by emphasizing the positive impact on patient care and operational efficiency.

- Deployment and monitoring: Full launch while implementing robust monitoring systems to track AI performance over time. Regularly update and maintain the AI models to ensure they remain relevant and effective. Establish mechanisms for collecting feedback from healthcare professionals and patients.

By systematically rolling out AI implementation according to plan, healthcare managers can enhance the adoption and integration of AI technologies in their organization.

## INTEGRATION AND ADOPTION STRATEGIES

Ensuring the accountability of AI within healthcare necessitates identifying the individuals accountable for the decisions driven by AI. This involves specifying the responsibilities of AI developers, healthcare providers and regulatory bodies. The establishment of resilient governance frameworks that can adapt to the dynamic landscape of AI technology will be pivotal in upholding accountability and fostering public trust. Health systems can facilitate the adoption of AI solutions through selected incentives, such as value-based payment schemes. When financial incentives are correctly aligned with patient outcomes and cost effectiveness, healthcare organizations can be encouraged to invest in administrative AI to enhance the efficiency and quality of services, ultimately striving for a more innovative, accessible yet sustainable healthcare system.

## MEASURING PERFORMANCE: KPA AND KPIS

There are myriad criteria a hospital manager can apply to evaluate the effectiveness of an AI system and its impact on overall organization performance. In a conventional approach, managers make use of macro-key performance areas (KPAs) and a subset of key performance indicators (KPIs). This can be an excellent approach to evaluating the effectiveness of an AI system and its impact on overall performance. By monitoring these indicators, hospital managers can effectively measure the impact of AI on their organization and make informed decisions (data-driven decision-making) to further enhance performance and achieve strategic objectives. Regular assessment and adjustment of these metrics is essential for ensuring ongoing success and improvement in healthcare delivery, as seen in the roadmap for AI implementation illustrated in this chapter.

As a quick recap, KPAs are broad areas or domains of activity within a healthcare organization that are crucial for achieving organizational goals and mission. Examples are quality improvement, patient care and resource management. Differently, KPIs are metrics for evaluating a KPA. Quantifiable data can aid managers in tracking progress and identifying areas for improvement and are optimal for transparency and accountability within an organization (see Fig. 11).

| KPA nr. | Resource management |
|---|---|
| Dimension | Institutional |
| Description | Optimization of institutional resources available |
| KPA Weight | (%) |
| KPI surgery | 1. AI solution planning rate (%)<br>2. Surgical room utilization rate (%)<br>3. % surgery time of total time<br>4. % on time surgeries<br>5. Utilization rate staff (%)<br>6. ... |

*Source:* Adapted from Lega (2023).

**Fig. 11. Example of a KPA Table for Reviewing the Performance of AI in Surgical Planning.**

KPA and KPIs hold importance for the implementation of AI solutions, given the hurdles to adoption such as resistance to change or apprehension about investment costs and perceived value. Through the identification of high-impact KPIs related to cost savings and resource utilization, for example, managers can prioritize the AI initiatives that offer the greatest benefit to their organization. This strategic approach ensures that resources are allocated effectively to maximize the value derived from AI solutions. KPIs enable managers to demonstrate the value proposition of AI software to key stakeholders (e.g. clinicians, leadership board and patients). By quantifying the tangible benefits associated with AI implementation, and tracking these benefits over time, managers can build the confidence and support needed for continued investment in AI.

## THE HUMAN FACTOR

As mentioned above, implementation entails 'making things happen'. It involves designing and managing control systems, creating dashboards to measure and assess expected performance. They are milestones and check points that help leaders to keep the team and collaborators on track. The phases and roadmap described above may provide inspiration for leaders wanting to introduce AI into their health organization. Implementation is never straightforward, however. Professionals are known to be resistant and resilient to changes that affect their interests. They adopt strategies to protect the status quo, as described by Ackroyd et al. (Ackroyd et al., 1989) with the term 'custodial orientation'. This suggests a form of management practice that is encapsulated by professional interests and primarily focused on maintaining the status quo (as defined by the professional community), especially if they sense a major risk or threat to their status, autonomy, power, such as the AI revolution might bring after an initial period of superficial acceptance. If the professionals feel empowered, so much the better. But what happens if they suspect their power base is at stake? In this light, planning stages and content of change might not be sufficient to generate the desired change. Leaders will need to cope with change management processes and go through three fundamental steps (Schein, 1965):

1. Unfreezing – the process of disrupting the habitual behaviour of employees. It may happen through the provision and sharing of information or through more enforcing tools (e.g. norms, financial incentives, rewards and punishments). This action involves communication and sharing of the need for change. People must perceive a sense of urgency for change. In other words, since people are not in the market for solutions until they recognize that there is a problem, the need for change should be made obvious to everybody and not just to the organization's top management.
2. Substituting – the replacement of old with new behaviour. The involvement of team members in defining new behaviour enhances support to change. From another perspective, it is impossible for a few people in senior positions to work out all the answers themselves.
3. Refreezing – the process of institutionalization of the new behaviour. This implies bringing positive outcomes to the attention of everyone and reinforcing new behaviour patterns. The goal is to re-establish the comfort level that employees experienced before the change.

Implementation is where leaders combine leadership qualities – for building engagement – with managerial capacities to drive the process forward. Managing change also means eschewing so-called simplicity traps, avoiding implementers who make sense of their task by concentrating on a narrow set of factors and removing the complications that impede full change (Weick, 1979). Such selective attention can, however, overemphasize some aspects of change and underestimate others, resulting in failure of the overall change. Leaders must control the 'whole picture', while working with the 'black box' of health service delivery processes, for which AI is deeply challenging.

Whenever leaders of health organizations launch change-development processes, they are managing complex change in strongly interconnected envisioning-implementation activities. Implementing AI starts with the key questions of why and what makes AI valuable for an organization or what makes it valuable for a specific unit, department, discipline, process and professional role? But the 'why' is always the starting point, the 'unfreezing', the trigger. Why us, why now?

This is always the starting point, the one that leaders can't miss if they want to prepare their organization for effective and durable implementation of AI. Once the why is clear, as well as the urgency to look at the rationale for the introduction of AI, then leaders can concentrate on which type of AI should be tested and implemented. They should 'walk the talk', that is, promote the adoption of AI systems consistent with the why. In essence, 'You do what you said you would do'.

Having done with these preparatory actions, comprising organizational assessment (Fig. 10), the remaining phases along the roadmap can be undertaken and managed.

## FINAL THOUGHTS ON LEADERSHIP POSTURE FOR EXCELLENT IMPLEMENTATION OF AI

Leaders who want to drive the AI revolution should have a leadership posture: a set of meta-expectations for the exercise of their role. They are expected to deliver performance and results, but how can they contribute to the search for improvement change in their organization? There is ample literature on leadership style, behaviour and best practices, just as there are approaches that distinguish great from good leaders in activities that combine a visionary capacity with a pragmatic focus on how to bring about extraordinary change. Leaders can help their organizations to become better places in many ways. But because of the approaches and actions they take in their leadership posture, they make the difference by their capacity to sustain efforts to develop an organizational culture of excellence and continuous improvement and change. A culture based on constant effort to cope with the three major pathological dynamics that affect all types of organizations (Khan & Lega, 2021):

- The focus on 'problemistic-search' decision-making.
- The attractive trap of 'satisficing'.
- The strong path dependency or 'retention of solution'.

Problemistic search refers to situations in which the search for alternatives is triggered when the organization encounters a problem (Cyert & March, 1963; March & Simon, 1958). It describes a behaviourally plausible process by which organizations can learn from performance feedback. When organizations realize that their performance is falling behind expectations, this awareness could lead to search for a solution to the problem, resulting in change to restore performance to the expected level.

Problemistic search draws on reactive behaviour. If and only if the problem is perceived as such, that is, awareness and urgency are recognized, then action will be taken. Conversely, good leaders are expected to take a proactive posture. Issues need to be addressed before they become problems. That is exactly what AI requires today – immediate and focused attention.

Satisficing is what sets great leaders apart. Satisficing is a decision-making strategy that aims to achieve a satisfactory or adequate result rather than the optimal solution. Instead of putting maximum effort towards attaining the best outcome, satisficing leads to adopting a minimalist approach to achieving the first attainable resolution that meets basic acceptable outcomes and ensues in quick solutions, shortcuts and low performance levels. Satisficing narrows the scope of options available to achieve those outcomes, setting aside options that would call for more intensive, complex or unfeasible efforts in the attempt to attain optimal results. This is because aiming for the optimal solution may necessitate an inordinate expenditure of time, energy and resources, which the organization (its leaders and managers) is unwilling to spend. Satisficing often results in so-called 'garbage can' decision-making.

The implication for health organization leaders is the expectation that they act as a driving force in raising performance thresholds – even beyond what is expected by the management by objectives (MbO) system. Leaders are expected to be ambitious. For themselves, the team they manage and their organization. Servant leaders continuously push the organization to challenge its performance. Again, introducing and implementing AI need to be a strategic component of the collective ambition of any health organization that wants to perform above average in the near future. Therefore, an ambition itself of the leading team.

Finally, retention of solutions refers to the natural tendency to search for solutions to problems from past experience. Organizations, like people, are pushed by the past rather than pulled by the future. However, we expect leaders to be naturally inclined to explore innovations, to benchmark against competitors and to infuse their organization with the latest trends, which includes studying others and adopting positive and lateral thinking. Clinical leaders attend scientific society meetings where they are informed of the latest in innovative technology and practices, yet they don't attend the meetings addressing organizational issues. This is precisely where more can be expected of them: curiosity about the changes in the way services are delivered, about trends in organizational transformation, about opportunities to re-think the way things are organized and managed. And AI can contribute to many aspects of the dynamics of healthcare organizations, from clinical decision-making to administration and from operations management to human resource management. Now is the time for leaders of healthcare organizations to explore AI. *Hic et nunc*.

## REFERENCES

Ackroyd, S., Hughes, J. A., & Soothill, K. (1989). Public sector services and their management. *Journal of Management Studies*, 26(6), 603–619. https://doi.org/10.1111/j.1467-6486.1989.tb00747.x

Cyert, R., & March, J. (1963). *A behavioural theory of the firm*. Prentice Hall.

Khan, U., & Lega, F. (2021). *Health Management 2.0*. Emerald Publishing Limited. https://doi.org/10.1108/9781800433427

Lega, F. (2023). *Economia e management sanitario. Settore, sistema, aziende, protagonisti*. EGEA.

Lesser, R., & Schweizer, C. (2024, January 23). Davos reflections and the road ahead. *BCG's Weekly Briefs*. https://www.bcg.com/about-us/about-bcg/weekly-briefs#:~:text=Our%20research%20shows%20that%209,we%20use%20the%20technology%20responsibly

March, J. G., & Simon, H. A. (1958). *Organizations*. Wiley.

NHS. (2019). *Preparing the healthcare workforce to deliver the digital future the Topol Review an independent report on behalf of the Secretary of State for Health and Social Care*. https://topol.hee.nhs.uk/wp-content/uploads/HEE-Topol-Review-2019.pdf

Schein, E. H. (1965). Organizational psychology. Prentice-Hall.

Weick, K. E. (1979). The social psychology of organizing. *M@n@gement*, *18*, 189–193. McGraw-Hill. https://doi.org/10.3917/mana.182.0189

Youssef, A., Ng, M. Y., Long, J., Hernandez-Boussard, T., Shah, N., Miner, A., Larson, D., & Langlotz, C. P. (2023). Organizational factors in clinical data sharing for artificial intelligence in health care. *JAMA Network Open*, 6(12), e2348422. https://doi.org/10.1001/jamanetworkopen.2023.48422

# AFTERWORD: WHY AI IS RELEVANT FOR CLINICAL LEADERS

We live in a world that is evolving at a speed with which humanity cannot keep a steady pace. So, too, technology and medical knowledge progress. In this context, it has become increasingly difficult to manage healthcare facilities operating a service model based on scientific methods and medical evidence that make the use of technology a necessity both clinically and managerially.

AI refers to technologies that can simulate human abilities such as reasoning and creativity. It is a short leap to recognizing AI as an extension of the human brain in its ability to provide tangible game-changing support for managing the peculiarities of medical practice. AI has brought benefit to healthcare. Diverse specialties are exploring its use in diagnosis and therapy and for aiding diagnosis in such fields as mine – interventional radiology. When viewed from a holistic perspective, the potential of AI in healthcare and medicine holds promise for clinical specialties and for the managerial and administrative areas that form the backbone of a healthcare system.

Within the complexity of the Italian healthcare system, AI may prove an essential tool to achieve the goals of public and private healthcare, while ensuring the system's sustainability despite the depletion of available resources. In a given hospital department, administrative AI applications could optimize the planning of work shifts. Moreover, AI could estimate in real-time resources used and available and automatically handle procurement and management, thus avoiding errors of human management. Additionally, rapid access to the knowledge of a specific disease, combined with the data of a specific patient, could further the goals of personalization of therapy and individual management, ultimately improving the quality of care.

AI support is also advantageous for managing the countless administrative tasks that absorb an inordinate amount of time and effort of doctors and nurses and that cause errors, stress and burnout. Furthermore, AI can recognize patterns within massive amounts of data more efficiently than a human can, owing to its computational capacity and ability to work beyond the usual eight-hour shift. In research and development, AI can help in the search for new drugs and the development of novel technologies.

There are no areas in healthcare within which the implementation of AI is not genuinely crucial. An interesting thought exercise is to try to imagine the impact of AI on diverse medical specialties. From the hospital department to the medical directorate, many activities could benefit from AI support. Envisioning a manager's work in healthcare is complex because the hospital is a multifaceted reality that staff and patients experience in very different ways.

Nonetheless, there are transversal medical and non-medical activities shared by all managerial fields. Reporting is one such activity. Awareness of what is happening is crucial for making informed decisions. AI can provide in-depth reporting, thus keeping management updated. Furthermore, AI can also synthetize data and present them in an appropriate fashion, thus reducing the time spent reading superfluous information. The possibility of error, aside from human supervision, could also be minimized.

Another typical managerial characteristic is possession of a sound knowledge of rules, laws and regulations, along with the ability to contextualize one's activity within regulatory frameworks. Given the amount of data involved, errors can occur, and valuable time may be spent verifying regulations to prevent oversights and mistakes. AI could support managers by working as an updated database with the capacity of synthesizing information, also the most recent, as effectively as possible. Making decisions is a key managerial activity, and making informed decisions is more necessary than ever before. Rapid access to information, coupled with the ability of AI applications to interpret data, would provide managers with predictions and visualization of hypothetical scenarios based on real-time hospital data. AI could help improve clinical practice and optimize the quality of a clinical leader's work by enhancing human relationships and reducing stress. AI applications hold promise for creating a better working environment for clinical leaders and their teams.

Printed and bound by CPI Group (UK) Ltd, Croydon, CR0 4YY
04/09/2024
14551128-0001